The Five Minute Parent

Fun & Fast Activities
for You and Your Little Ones

Deborah Shelton
Illustrated by Frankie Gordon

Cover Design by George Foster
Back Cover Writing by Susan Kendrick

First Edition 10 9 8 7 6 5 4 3 2

Printed in the United States of America
Published by Bayou Publishing
2524 Nottingham, Houston, TX 77005
Phone: 713-526-4558
www.BayouPublishing.com

Library of Congress Catalog Card Number: 2001132542

Publisher's Cataloging-in-Publication
(Provided by Quality Books, Inc.)

Shelton, Deborah (Deborah L.)
  The five minute parent : fun & fast activities for you and your little ones / Deborah Shelton ; illustrated by Frankie Gordon. -- 1st.
  p. cm.
  Includes index.
  ISBN 1-886298-13-0

  1. Family recreation. 2. Games. 3. Cookery.
4. Handicraft. I. Gordon, Frankie. II. Title.

GV182.7.S54 2002   790.1'91
                    QBI02-701527

Dedication:

This book is for my beautiful son Kizer,

who has shown me that time spent with him

is one thing I will never regret.

What People Are Saying About The Five Minute Parent

"This is a wonderful book and I am sure any parent or caregiver could use it over and over again. I am a coordinator of a resource center and the activities are just the kind we could use for our students. Thanks!"
—Linda Cross
Coordinator, Reiley Family Resource Center, Alexandria, Kentucky

"I wish I had this book when my children were young—but now I have it for when the grandchildren come to visit."
—Connie Dean, Mother of 5, Grandmother of 6

"*The Five Minute Parent* is a book every parent of young children should have in their home. An instant boredom buster that stimulates creativity and learning!"
—Heidi Hoff, Publisher of Preschool Planet

"If you want an enriching experience, share the projects in *The Five Minute Parent* with your child. You will both grow in the process."
—Jane Jacobs, Program Director,
Special Programs Organized Recreational Therapy (S.P.O.R.T.), City of LaPorte, Texas

"The interesting thing is that there are activities that my 12 year old can do, as well as ones for her younger brothers. My wife and I especially like the cost effectiveness of the activities. The kids have fun, we have fun and everybody is happy!
—Manuel Cuevas, Father of 3

"A creative complement to homeschool curriculum."
—Martha Jenke, Homeschooling Mother of 4

"As a long-time home educator, I appreciate the easy-to-use ideas in this warm-hearted book. *The Five Minute Parent* is one of those resources I wish I'd had available to me when my own three children were preschool age. How much fun today's parents will have now that Deborah Shelton's book is on the market!"
—Deborah Taylor-Hough, Editor of Bright-Kids newsletter

"I want to take this book with me to all of my babysitting jobs!"
—Kimberly Romero, age 14

"Wonderful, practical ideas for turning the desire for quality fun time with kids into a reality!"
—Anne Grizzle, LMSW-ACP, Family Therapist

"This book is a godsend to a homeschooling parent. I love the fact that it reminded me to do fun things with my kids (not just make their schooling fun and interesting) so that I'm also a parent who does cool things with them in addition to a mom who's teaching them daily."
—Jannai Phelps, Homeschooling Mother of 4

"This is a recipe for fun!"
—Kandace Savitsky, Devoted Aunt of 8

Introduction

I will never forget the day I decided to write this book. My 2 $\frac{1}{2}$-year-old son and I were at home together, in the office. I sat at one end of the desk, staring at the computer screen, watching the cursor race as my finger tapped furiously on the backspace key, while my son sat at the opposite end, watching the portable television. My latest parenting article was no match for the dreaded Writer's Block. "Mommy, I want to go camping," my son interrupted.

Without taking my eyes from the screen, I answered, "Not right now Sweetie. Mommy's working now...maybe this weekend," and continued typing.

"But I want to go camping *now* Mommy!" he wailed. I turned to see tears on the verge of spilling over his cheeks. He kept pointing at the television, which featured a happy sitcom family enjoying a camping trip in the woods. I looked at the tears again, then shot a glance at the computer screen. "Finding Time for 'Quality' Time" was all that had survived the backspace key.

That's when it hit me: Don't wait for the weekend! Five short minutes later, my son and I transformed our living room into a sofa-cushion-and-bed-sheet camping ground. He was thrilled, we had a ton of fun, and I subsequently defeated Writer's Block.

The Five Minute Parent is for parents, grandparents, teachers, caregivers and families. Most of all, it is for children who want to see and experience their world NOW, and for adults who catch themselves saying, "Maybe this weekend". Have you ever noticed how many things in our lives get put off until the weekend? *The Five Minute Parent* is not only about finding more time to spend with our children, but also finding more creative ways to spend the time we already have.

The activities in *The Five Minute Parent* are ideal for play dates, rainy-day blues busting, and overall family fun. Most of the projects call for materials that you probably already have in your home. If not, use that as an excuse to visit your favorite craft supply store.

At the back of this book, you will find a comprehensive index that lists the activities by their names and also by their materials. The appendix offers a brief directory of parent resource centers by state. Parent resource centers provide support in the form of counseling, parent training classes, special needs assistance, family literacy programs and much more.

I hope you enjoy this book, and remember: Don't wait for the weekend! No matter how hectic your schedule, you can create small treasures and lasting memories with your children in just minutes!

Have fun!

Deborah Shelton

Contents

Household items to save:
- coffee cans
- cardboard tubes
  (from paper towels, wrapping paper, etc.)
- metal pie tins
- shoeboxes
- baby food jars
- plastic soda bottles
- compact discs
- magazines
  (for cut-outs)

1: Getting Organized

Have the right supplies (and know where they are)!

Having a craft supply box readily available is essential for completing any project—not to mention those that require only a few minutes to complete. The most convenient option is to stock a small bookshelf with the following containers and materials:

Plastic Bins or Shoeboxes:
Fill with crayons, felt scraps, fabric, magazine cut-outs, glue, tape, bottles of paint, etc.

Coffee Cans:
Place paintbrushes, markers, popsicle sticks, and pipe cleaners (chenille stems) in decorated coffee cans. Use different sizes of cans to hold different materials.

Baby Food Jars:
Small items such as beads, buttons and googly eyes fit neatly into baby food jars, which can be stored together in a shoebox.

Empty Shelf:
Save a space for pads of construction paper, newspapers and magazines.

Clear Top Shelf:
A clear top shelf works well as a "drying table" for paint projects.

Shoe Bag:
If space is limited, use a clear plastic shoe bag, hung on the back of a door, to hold your supplies.

Clean Up:
Make clean-up easy by keeping rolls of paper towels, sheets of newsprint, rubber gloves for paint projects, and a bag of sponges stored together.

Also, teach children the importance of cleaning up by incorporating the clean-up as part of the activity. Delegate by having one child in charge of all paper and drawing supplies; another handles the fabric and felt scraps, and so on. Make sure that there is a place for everything, so you can spend time having fun instead of searching for missing materials.

A few creative ways to display your works of art:

• The Refrigerator Hall of Fame
This type of display will always be a favorite!

• Clothesline Art
Attach a string across a wall and attach art with clothespins.

• Family Art Club
Too many works of art to display? Make a list of family members who would enjoy receiving your child's creations. Send them a new piece every month!

• Gallery Opening
Place artwork on plate stands, or propped against windows and invite family and friends over to view your exhibit!

2: Adventures In Art

Add vibrant color to everything in your life!

Sand Scribbles

Materials: construction paper or poster board
colored sand
bottle of glue

Directions: Squeeze the glue onto the paper in letters (child's name), a picture or wacky design. Now sprinkle colored sand on top of the glue. Shake off the excess sand and allow to dry. This project is addictive, so instead of keeping all of them, give a few of your sand scribbles to family and friends.

Fun & Fast Fact
Many Native American Indians, such as the Navaho tribe, used colored sands to make intricate and beautiful designs.

Painting Press

Materials: 2 sheets of 8 ½" x 11" waxed paper (or cut to fit the size of paper you use) construction paper or typing paper non-toxic finger paint

Directions: Fingerpaint designs onto a sheet of waxed paper. Place another sheet of waxed paper on top and press down gently, squishing the colors together. Peel the top layer off, then press onto a sheet of construction paper. Remove the waxed paper. You can make several prints from one wax painting. With your own painting press, the possibilities are endless!

Fun & Fast Tip
Use the painting press to make your own holiday greeting cards or party invitations.

Handprint Art

Materials: tempera paint or finger paint
paper plate
construction paper

Directions: Pour a thin layer of paint onto a paper plate. Press your hand into the paint, covering the entire palm. Now press your hand onto a piece of construction paper. Be creative by making handprint turkeys for Thanksgiving; colorful butterflies; or a collage of hands.

Fun & Fast Tip
Measure your growth by making a new piece of handprint art each month or each year. Don't forget to write the date on them!

Tissue Paper Collage

Materials: construction paper (or coloring book pages)
pencil
sheets of different colored tissue paper
glue

Directions: First, draw a picture on the construction paper. For a faster project, or for much younger children, use a page from a favorite coloring book. Instead of coloring the picture with crayons, tear off bits of colored tissue paper, crumple, and glue the pieces to the picture.

Fun & Fast Tip
Make this project easier for toddlers by tracing the outlines of the coloring book page with glue.

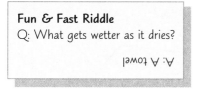

Fun & Fast Riddle
Q: What gets wetter as it dries?

A: A towel

Splitter-Splatters

Materials: tempera paint
paintbrush
paper plate
spray bottle filled with water (optional)

Directions: Paint designs and pictures onto the paper plate, using a paintbrush or your fingers. Hold the plate, painted side up, in the rain. A few big drops of rain will go a long way, so don't hold it out too long. If you want to try this project on a sunny day, fill a spray bottle with water and spray your painting until the colors begin to run together. Set the plate on a level surface to dry. A rainy-day favorite!

22

Seashell Memories

Materials: clean seashells
acrylic paints
paintbrush

Directions: Preserve your memories of the beach by painting pictures on the inside of the seashells that you collected. What did you see at the beach? Fish, a lighthouse, boats, and palm trees painted on the shells will make great reminders of your trip to the ocean!

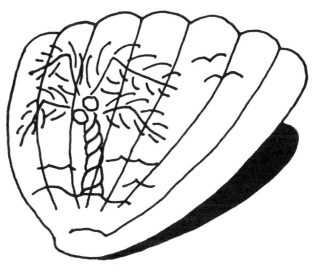

Fun & Fast Riddle
Q: Why do seagulls only fly over the sea?

A: Because if they flew over the bay, they'd be bagels!

23

Rocky Colors

Materials: rocks in various shapes and sizes
acrylic paints
paintbrush

Directions: Gather different shapes and sizes of rocks from your neighborhood and paint funny faces on them, or wild and colorful designs. Rocky Colors make cute and creative paperweight gifts.

Fun & Fast Joke
Q: What rock group has 4 men that don't sing?

A: Mount Rushmore!

24

Creative Faces

Materials: washable, non-toxic paints
paintbrush

Directions: Dip the paintbrush into the paint and draw designs on your face! Simple designs and pictures, such as a lady bug or a smiley face, work best. Be careful not to get paint near your eyes or mouth. This is a big hit at birthday parties!

Fun & Fast Quote
"Only your real friends will tell you when your face is dirty."
-Sicilian Proverb

Smooch Picture

Materials: paper
lipstick
crayons

Directions: First, apply dark lipstick to your lips. Next, "kiss" the paper in the middle of the page. Draw the face and features (eyes, nose, etc.) around the lips. This is a fun way to draw family portraits!

Fun & Fast Tip
This is a fun activity for play dates, too. Make sure each child uses a different tube of lipstick to prevent the spread of icky germs.

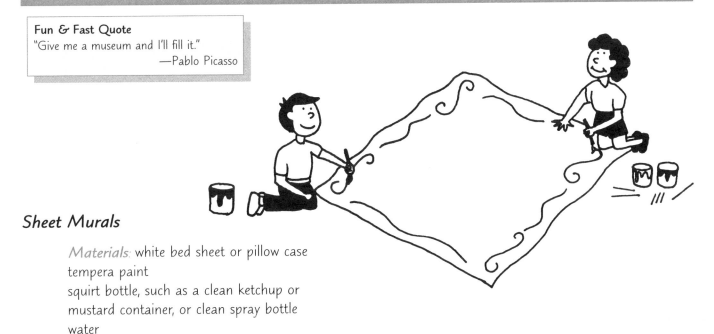

Sheet Murals

Materials: white bed sheet or pillow case
tempera paint
squirt bottle, such as a clean ketchup or
mustard container, or clean spray bottle
water

Directions: Hang your canvas (sheet or pillow case) on a clothesline. Fill a squirt bottle or spray bottle with water and add just enough paint to color the water and not clog the spray. Shake well to mix. Stand a few feet away from the sheet and create your next masterpiece! *Note: If you're doing this project indoors, be sure to use a drop cloth.

Really into science? Check out these websites!

• Science Made Simple
www.sciencemadesimple.com

• Cool Science for Curious Kids
www.hhmi.org/coolscience

• The Science Club
www.halcyon.com/sciclub/kidproj1.html

• NASA Kids
http://kids.msfc.nasa.gov

• Funology—The Science of Having Fun!
www.funology.com

3: Weird & Wacky Science Experiments

Amaze friends and family with your scientific knowledge!

Tornado In a Jar

Materials: clean glass jar with lid
water
dishwashing liquid
food coloring (optional)

Directions: Fill the jar with water and add a few drops of dishwashing liquid. Next, put a few drops of food coloring into the jar. Place the lid on tight and swirl the jar in a circular motion several times. Stop and look inside. You should see a mini tornado!

Fun & Fast Fact
A *waterspout* is a tornado that occurs over a lake or ocean.

Moo Juice Science

Materials: milk (moo juice)
pie tin or shallow baking dish
dishwashing liquid
food coloring

Directions: Cover the bottom of the dish with milk. Next, add a drop or two of food coloring, but don't stir. Now add a few drops of dishwashing liquid. Can you believe your eyes? The dishwashing liquid broke the surface tension of the milk.

Fun & Fast Trivia
Q: What color is yak milk?
A: Pink!

Egg In a Bottle

Materials: clean soda or juice bottle (glass)
hard-boiled egg (peeled)
strips of newspaper
matches

Directions: Place small strips of newspaper into the bottle. Light the strips on fire by dropping in a lit match (adult supervision required). When the paper begins to burn, place the egg over the opening of the bottle, and wait. Soon the egg will fall into the bottle with a loud POP! The fire from the match consumed the oxygen inside the bottle, which created a vacuum and caused the egg to be pushed inside.

Fun & Fast Quote
"Put all your eggs in the one basket and—watch that basket!"
—Mark Twain

Floating Needle

Materials: clean drinking glass
water
newsprint
sewing needle

Directions: Fill a glass with water, then float a piece of newsprint on the surface. Don't let the edges dip under the water. Next, place a needle on top of the newsprint. Slowly dip the edges of the paper into the water until the paper sinks and the needle is left floating. Now, touch the water and watch the needle sink. This is a great way to teach children about surface tension.

Fun & Fast Trivia
Q: What is the fear of pins and needles called?

A: Belonephobia

Bending Water

Materials: plastic comb
water faucet

Directions: Turn on the cold water in your kitchen sink, letting the water run out in a small, steady stream. Run the comb through dry hair several times to charge it. Slowly bring the charged comb near the stream of water. How did the comb make the water "bend"? The water was neutral, not charged, and was attracted to the charged comb and moved toward it! Amazing!

Fun & Fast Riddle
Q: What has teeth but no mouth?

A: A comb

Slimey Goop

Materials: 1 tsp laundry detergent powder
1 cup of water
2 cups white glue
food coloring
large plastic bowl with lid

Directions: Combine laundry powder and water in the plastic bowl. Add the glue and stir the mixture with your hands until it forms a gooey ball. Your slimey goop can be any color you want it to be, just by adding a few drops of food coloring. Store the goop in an airtight plastic container until you're ready to play with it again. Squish your fingers into the mixture for gooey fun.

Fun & Fast Joke
Q: Why did the slimey goop cross the road?

A: Because it was stuck to my shoe!

Chemical Balloon

Materials: clean soda or juice bottle
(glass)
1 balloon
small funnel
vinegar
baking soda

Directions: Use the funnel to pour 2 tablespoons of baking soda into the bottle. Now pour in roughly $1/3$ cup of vinegar. Put the balloon over the mouth of the bottle fast! Swirl the bottle just a bit to get things started. Vinegar mixed with baking soda produces CO_2 (carbon dioxide gas), which fills the balloon.

Fun & Fast Fact
The world's record for the most balloons blown up and tied in 1 hour belongs to K.C. Williams, at 468 balloons!

Fun & Fast Fact
Craven Walker is known as the inventor and "Father" of liquid motion lamps.

Wave Maker

Materials: clear plastic soda or water bottle (2-liter works best)
small funnel
food coloring (two different colors)
vegetable oil
water
electrical tape
glitter (optional)

Directions: Use the funnel to fill the bottle half way full with water. Add 3-4 drops of each color of food coloring. Add a few pinches of glitter (optional). Use the funnel to fill the rest of the bottle with vegetable oil. Screw the cap on AS TIGHT AS POSSIBLE. Wrap the cap with electrical tape to prevent small leaks. Gently rock and tilt the bottle from side to side to create waves!

Coin Overflow

Materials: drinking glass
water
coins

Directions: Fill a glass to the brim with water. Try to guess the number of coins that will cause the water to overflow. Slowly drop coins in, one at a time. Count how many coins it takes to make the water spill out. How close was your guess to the actual number of coins?

Fun & Fast Trivia

Q: Who was the first woman to appear on United States currency?

A: Martha Washington. She appeared on $1 silver certificates in 1886, 1891 and 1896.

Fun & Fast Fact
Bubbles are round because the air inside pushes equally against all its parts, causing all points on the surface to be of equal distance from the center.

Bubbles

Materials: dishwashing liquid
corn syrup
water
jar or bowl

Directions: This is super easy and super fun! Just mix a small amount of dishwashing liquid and corn syrup into a jar of water, dip your bubble blower into the mixture, and start blowing! To make your own bubble blowers, see Chapter 6: Family Fun Time, page 72, or Chapter 12: Outside Fun Guide, page 146 for a giant bubble blower.

Share your love of writing with a pen pal!

- Kid City Kid's Mailbox
  www.child.net/kidsmail.htm

- Keypals Club International
  www.worldkids.net/clubs/kci

- Kidsnews.com Penpals
  www.kidnews.com/penpals.html

- KidsCom
  www.kidscom.com

4: Writing and Wishing You Were Here

Design your own books and bookmarks! Keep in touch with family and friends with original postcards and letters!

Felt Story Board

Materials: shoebox with lid
felt
flannel (optional)
glue
scissors

Directions: First, cut a piece of felt or flannel to fit snugly inside the lid of the shoebox. As a background, light blue works well. Glue the flannel to the inside of the lid. Cut pieces of felt into shapes to make people. For example, use circles for heads and small rectangles for arms and legs, or cut out complete people and animals to suit your child's favorite story book. Once the pieces are cut, let the story begin! When you're finished playing, store the pieces inside the shoebox. Felt story boards are also a great way to teach numbers and letters of the alphabet to young children.

Fun & Fast Quote
"Why do writers write? Because it isn't there.
—Thomas Berger

Fun & Fast Quote
"In the book of life,
the answers aren't in the back."
—Charlie Brown

Flip Books

Materials: small pad of paper (Post-it® pads work well)
pencil or pen

Directions: First, choose something to "animate" such as a bouncing ball or a plant growing from a seed. Start drawing on the last piece of paper in the note pad. If you're drawing a plant, you could begin with a small seed under the ground. In the next frame, draw the seed again, but with a small sprout growing. The next frame, and so on, will show the seedling growing into a full-grown flower. To see your creation, put your thumb on the edge of the note pad and flip through the pages quickly. Your very own "moving" picture!

My Color Books

Materials: white construction paper for the book same colored materials for inside of book (for a pink book use pink cotton, pink ribbons pink stickers, etc.)
glue
scissors
markers

Directions: Fold the construction paper in half to form the book. Glue colored materials to the inside of the book. Use ribbons, stickers, cloth, glitter, etc., to create "blue" books, "red" books, "purple" books, and so on. Label the front "My (Blue) Book." Learn colors the fun way!

Fun & Fast Fact
The Diamond Sutra, a religious book printed in China in AD 868, is the earliest dated printed book in the world.

Letter Puzzles

Materials: writing paper
pen or markers
scissors
envelope
postage stamp

Directions: First, write a letter to Grandma and Grandpa or a friend who lives far away. Cut the letter into large, connecting puzzle pieces. Now place the pieces into the envelope, stamp and address the outside, and mail! In order to read your letter, the receiver has to put the puzzle together first!

Fun & Fast Fact
Our English alphabet has 26 letters; *Rotokas*, a language spoken in the South Pacific, only has 11; the Russian language has 33; the Hebrew alphabet has 27; and the Cambodian alphabet has a whopping 72 letters!

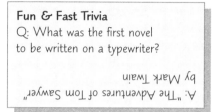

Fun & Fast Trivia
Q: What was the first novel
to be written on a typewriter?

A: "The Adventures of Tom Sawyer"
by Mark Twain

Book Name Plates

Materials: large self-adhesive
postal labels
colored markers
ink stamp and pad or stickers

Directions: First, use colored markers to write a dedication in the center of the label. For example: This book belongs to; This book is a gift from. Leave space for the recipient to write her name. Decorate the name plate with a border of stamp prints or colorful stickers. Book name plates add a personal touch when giving books as gifts.

"Wish You Were Here" Postcards

Materials: blank index cards
postage stamp
markers
crayons

Directions: On the left half of the stamped side of the card, write a brief message to a friend or family member. On the right half of the same side, address the postcard. On the other side of the card, write the title "Wish You Were Here" and draw a picture of your house, backyard, or the shape of your state with a star indicating where you are. Drop it in the mailbox and let someone know how much they are missed.

Fun & Fast Trivia
Q: What is the only 15-letter word in the English language that can be spelled without repeating a letter?

A: uncopyrightable

47

Touch and Feel Book

Materials: construction paper or card stock
materials of different textures (sandpaper; cotton balls; velvet; bubble wrap; plastic; felt; waxed paper)
glue
stapler

Directions: Glue one textured material per page of construction paper. Staple the pages together. Have your child close her eyes and tell you what each feels like—rough, soft, etc. Young children will enjoy discovering the many textures of the world around them.

Fun & Fast Fact
Sandpaper was invented in 1834.
Bubble wrap debuted in 1957.
Thomas Edison came up with waxed paper in 1872.

Bedroom Mailboxes

Materials: large manila envelope
small spiral note pad (pocket-size)
pencil
yarn
2 thumbtacks

Directions: Attach the envelope, length-wise, to the outside of your bedroom door, with a thumbtack. Push the tack through the flap of the envelope, near the top, with the opening toward you. This is your mailbox, and you can decorate it. Next, thread a piece of yarn through the spiral binding of the notepad, form a loop and knot the ends together. Store a pencil through the spiral. Secure another thumbtack to the door and hang the note pad from it. Family members can write quick notes to each other and place them in the mailbox. A creative way to keep in touch or say 'I love you.'

Fun & Fast Riddle
Q: What starts with a P, ends with an E, and has a million letters in it?

A: Post Office!

Family Quote Book

Materials: small notebook
pen

Directions: Record all of the witty things that your family members say! Write down the quote, who said it, and the date. For example: "We have more bills than a duck farm!"—Dad, July 7, 2001. "Well, that's the way the mop flops."—Mom, August 14, 2001. At the end of each week or month, share some of your favorites with the family, around the dinner table.

Fun & Fast Fact
Not everyone reads from left to right. The Japanese language is read top-to-bottom, and the Arabic language is read from right to left.

CanYouReadThisWay?

?sihT ekiL tuobA woH

Life Guessing

Materials: silliness

Directions: This is a fun and easy project. Sit on a park bench and make up a story about the next person who walks by. Notice their clothes and how fast or slow they walk. What does the person do for a living? Where are they going? Where did they just come from? Now, imagine that you are the person walking past. What story would someone else imagine about you?

**Are you a sports or games fanatic?
Check out these cool sites!**

• Sports Illustrated for Kids
  www.sikids.com

• Kids Domain Online Games
  www.kidsdomain.com/games

• Boowa & Kwala
  www.boowakwala.com

5: Games and Sports, of Sorts

Find new games to play, or enjoy some old favorites!

Balloon Tennis

Materials: paper plate
wooden paint stir stick or long cardboard tube
glue
balloon

Directions: Glue the wooden stir stick, or cardboard tube, to the paper plate to form the racket. Blow up a balloon and gently tap it with the racket. Tennis anyone?

Fun & Fast Fact
July is National Tennis Month. Celebrate by inviting friends over for a balloon tennis tournament!

Balloon Tap

Materials: balloons
string
small plant hooks or thumbtacks

Directions: Blow up 3 or 4 different colored balloons (do not use helium, because the balloons are not supposed to float). Tie string to each balloon and suspend them from the ceiling, using small plant hooks or thumbtacks. Let each one dangle to a different height. To play, let your toddler run and jump and tap each one. Turn on music for even more fun!

Fun & Fast Trivia

Q: Who were the first to travel in a hot-air balloon?

A: A duck, a rooster and a sheep flew by balloon for 8 minutes in September of 1783.

55

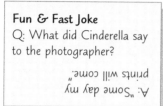

Picture Concentration

Materials: family photos (doubles needed)

Directions: For younger children, start with a smaller game using only 2 or 3 different photos (doubles of each). For older children, use 6 different photos (doubles needed, 12 pictures total). Lay the photos face down on the floor or on a table, in rows. Turn one picture over. Turn another photo over to find a match. If the two match, try to find another matching pair. If they don't match, turn the pictures over and try again. A new twist on a childhood favorite!

Fun & Fast Trivia
Q: If a rooster lays an egg on the very tip top of a house, which direction will the egg fall?

A: Roosters don't lay eggs!

Egg Walk

Materials: one uncooked egg
spoon
2 or more players

Directions: *This game has a huge mess potential, so be sure to place a drop cloth on the floor, or play this one outside. First, place the egg on the spoon. Balance is the key to this game. Walk across the yard to the next player, and hand the spoon to them. Be careful! Don't drop the egg! The next player walks to another player and hands the spoon to them, and so on. The winner is the player who isn't covered with egg goo.

Suitcase Relay Race

Materials: 2 suitcases
2 pair of adult-sized shoes
2 adult-sized shirts
2 pair of adult-sized shorts or pants
2 hats
at least 4 players (must be even number of players)

Directions: Place a set of clothes into each suitcase. Divide the children into 2 main teams. Divide each main team into 2 smaller groups, with one group a short distance from the other (the length of the relay). On the signal, one child from each competing group opens their suitcase and dresses completely; layering the game clothes over their own. All buttons should be buttoned and all shoes should be tied. Once dressed, the player closes the suitcase and carries it the length of the relay to their partner on the other side. Once there, remove the game clothes and close the suitcase. The child who is waiting, then repeats the entire process and runs across the relay to the next person. When all members of one team have dressed and undressed, they are declared the winners. You may want to videotape this, because it's so funny you'll want to watch it again and again!

Bottle Bowling

Materials: clean, empty 2-liter soda bottles (or smaller plastic bottles)
small plastic ball

Directions: Set the bottles in a row (side by side) or in other positions to make the game more challenging. Stand a few feet from the bottles, and roll the ball toward them in a gentle, underhand motion. Each player gets 2 chances to knock down all the bottles. When your turn is over, set the bottles into position for the next player. Tons of fun and no league membership required!

Fun & Fast Fact
The International Bowling Museum and Hall of Fame is located in St. Louis, Missouri.

59

Red Light/Green Light

Materials: 2 or more players

Directions: One person is designated as "IT." The other players should stand in a line, side by side, a fairly long distance from IT. To begin the game, IT turns his back to the players and says, "Green light!" When the players hear "green light" they walk as fast as they can toward IT and try to gain as much ground as possible. After a count of 5 or more, IT calls, "Red light!" and turns around to face the players. When the players hear "red light" they should stop immediately and freeze their positions. Any player still moving when IT turns around, must go back to the beginning. The first player to reach IT wins!

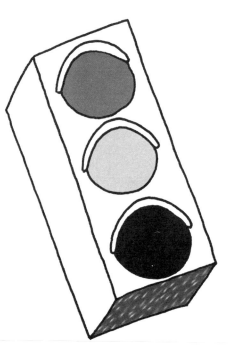

Fun & Fast Fact
The first traffic light, invented by Garrett Morgan, was installed in Cleveland, Ohio in 1914.

Simon Says

Materials: 2 or more players

Directions: One person is designated as "Simon." The other players stand in a line, side by side. The game starts when Simon says, "Simon says...(touch your nose; take one step forward; run in place)." The players only move when they hear, "Simon says..." If Simon says, "Take one step back," without saying, "Simon says..." it's a trick! Any player who moves when they don't hear, "Simon says..." is out of the game. The game ends when there is one player left. This is a fun way to fine-tune your listening skills!

Fun & Fast Quote
"Half this game is ninety percent mental."
—Yogi Berra

Where Is the Ball?

Materials: 3 plastic drinking cups
small ball

Directions: As your child watches, turn the cups upside-down, on their rims, and place the ball under one of the cups. Rearrange the cups quickly. Let your child try to guess which cup the ball is under. Is the hand quicker than the eye?

Fun & Fast Fact

In Sweden, it is against the law to train a seal to balance a ball on its nose.

62

Charades

Materials: scraps of paper
pencil
small box, bag or jar
several players

Directions: First, choose a theme such as Movies, Animals, People We Know, etc. Give a scrap of paper to each player and have them write something that matches the theme (the name of a movie, a kind of animal, a person you know, etc.). Place all of the scraps into a small box, bag or jar. Each player then picks a piece of paper from the collection and acts out the words on the paper while the other players try to guess what is written on the paper. Remember, no talking!

Possible Charades Themes:

- Popular Movies
- Occupations
- People We Know
- Foods We Love
- Historic Events
- Places We'd Like to Go
- Zoo Animals

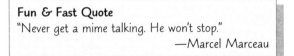

Fun & Fast Quote
"Never get a mime talking. He won't stop."
—Marcel Marceau

Great ideas for family fun on the Internet!

• Kids Jokes
  www.kidsjokes.co.uk

• Family Life Magazine
  www.FamilyLifeMag.com

• The Five Minute Parent
  www.fiveminuteparent.com

• The F.U.N. Place
  www.thefunplace.com

6: Family Fun Time

Family togetherness doesn't stop at the dinner table!

Movie Madness Party

Materials: mattress or
sleeping bags
pillows
blankets
television
VCR or DVD player
movies
snacks

Directions: Although the movie will last for 2 hours, setting up only takes 5 minutes. Remove the top mattress from your bed (Don't try this with a King size unless you have plenty of help and a strong back!), and place it in the middle of the floor. Add a blanket, every pillow in the house, and movie munchies, and you're in for 2 hours of fun!

1. Sally sells Seashells by the Seashore.
2. Rubber baby buggy bumpers.
3. Old oily Otto operates on old oily autos.

Fun & Fast Joke
Q: What breaks when you say it?

A: Silence!

Tenacious Tongue Twisters

Materials: silliness

Directions: You can make up your own tongue twisters by beginning each word of a sentence with the same letter, or you can laugh yourself silly with these:

Old oily Otto operates on old oily autos.

Silly Sally sings sweet songs softly.

Mom makes marshmallow munchies on Mondays.

Try to say your tongue twister very fast, 3 times. Ha ha ha ha ha!

67

Community Helper

Materials: gently worn clothing
toys
blankets
non-perishable food items

Directions: Spend 5 minutes each day preparing a box of gently worn clothing, toys and non-perishable food for a local homeless shelter. This teaches children the values of compassion and helping those who are less fortunate.

Fun & Fast Fact
The first Salvation Army kettle was used in San Francisco in 1891.

Today on the way to school, I saw a weird light in the sky. It flashed like a blinking Christmas bulb,

and dollars danced to me and jumped into my backpack!

then shot through the clouds and landed. It landed on top

Sentence Stories

Materials: pencil

paper

silliness

Directions: Sit around the kitchen table with the entire family. Choose someone to write down the sentences. The first person says a sentence: "Today on the way to school, I saw a weird light in the sky." The next person adds a new sentence to the first: "It flashed like a blinking Christmas bulb, then shot through the clouds and landed." Each person adds a new sentence, making the story a tall tale or just a funny and far-out narrative without rhyme or reason. When you're finished, read the story aloud to the entire family for even more laughs!

of the bank! Suddenly, the doors swung open and out jumped dancing money! Nickels and pennies, dimes

69

Indoor Camping

Materials: sofa cushions
flat sheets
towels
clothes pins or binder clips

Directions: First, remove the cushions from the sofa to form the 'perimeter' of your fort. Next, lay sheets and towels across the top of the cushions, and secure with clothespins or binder clips, if necessary. You can make this a real camping party by adding flashlights, telling scary stories, or making smores! Crawl in and let the fun begin!

Time In a Box

Materials: small plastic box with lid or shoebox
family photos
scissors
glue
markers
miscellaneous family mementos

Directions: Decorate the outside of your time capsule with family photos and label it "Our Family" and write the year. Fill the capsule with mementos such as baby pictures, ticket stubs, newspaper clippings, and any personal items that the family will enjoy seeing 5 or 10 years from now. Mom and Dad can hide the box in a safe, dry place inside the house, instead of burying it in the yard.

Fun & Fast Fact
A time capsule in Seward, Nebraska contains an automobile and a motorcycle! It is set to be opened in the year 2025.

Fun & Fast Fact
The world's record for the most people blowing
bubbles at the same time is 23,680 people!
It happened in Upton Park, London in May 1999.

Bubble Blowers

Materials: plastic drinking straws
(enough for everyone to have two)
scissors
tape
bubble solution (see page 39)

Directions: Cut 2 drinking straws in half. Next, tape the 4 pieces together, wrapping the tape around the middle. Dip the end into bubble solution and blow. This makes lots of tiny bubbles!

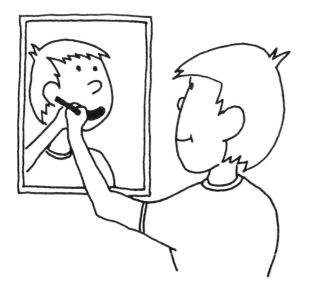

Face Trace

Materials: mirror
washable paints
paintbrush

Directions: Look into a mirror (works best with the medicine cabinet mirror in the bathroom). Using washable paints, "trace" your child's features—lips, nose, eyebrows, and hair onto the mirror. Have fun looking at your new self!

Fun & Fast Fact
It takes only 17 muscles to smile, but you use 43 to frown!

73

Fun & Fast Fact
S.O.S. does not stand for "Save Our Ship." The letters were chosen
because they are easy to send in Morse code—3 dots, 3 dashes, 3 dots.

Safety Day

Materials: sketch of your home
with exits marked
batteries

Directions: First, inspect all smoke and carbon monoxide detectors in your home, and replace all non-working batteries. Lead the family around the house, pointing out all the exits. Make sure that each family member knows where the exits are in case of a fire or other emergency. It's a good idea to photocopy the exit sketch, and display one in each bedroom and in the other rooms of your home. Some time during the day, when everyone is scattered around the house, yell "Fire drill!" and count the seconds it takes for everyone to get out of the home. This simple activity may prove to be a lifesaver.

Family First-Aid Kit

Materials: plastic container
such as a large fishing tackle box
bandages
rubbing alcohol
gauze
aspirin
elastic bandages
antiseptic
eye wash
tweezers
bandage scissors
red permanent marker

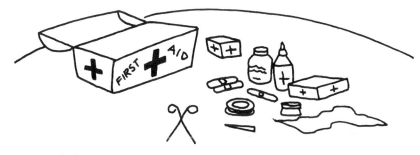

Directions: Spend a few minutes gathering materials for the first-aid kit. When you're finished, label the box in red permanent marker "First-Aid Kit." Keep this in a cabinet in the bathroom.

"People Who Love Me" List

Materials: paper
markers or pen

Directions: Sit down with your child and make a list of all the people who love her. (Parents, please limit yourself to 5 minutes for this project, because after all, doesn't *everyone* love our children? This project could take hours!) When you're finished, frame the list or have it laminated, then hang it in her bedroom. Have her refer to the list whenever she feels blue. It's a guaranteed mood lifter!

Fun & Fast Quote
"What the world really needs is more love and less paperwork."
—Pearl Bailey

Fun & Fast Quote
"Talk to a man about himself
and he will listen for hours."
—Benjamin Disraeli

Family Interviews

Materials: small tape recorder
with blank cassette or video camera with blank tape
list of questions

Directions: Spend five minutes interviewing each member of your family. Take your tape recorder or video camera to family reunions, birthday parties and sleepovers to interview as many relatives as possible. Sample questions: Which person do you most admire? When you were a child, what did you want to be when you grew up? This will make a very personal family keepsake.

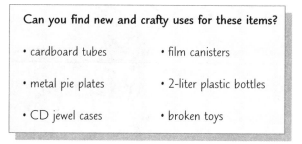

Can you find new and crafty uses for these items?

- cardboard tubes
- film canisters
- metal pie plates
- 2-liter plastic bottles
- CD jewel cases
- broken toys

She can do it; he can do it; you can do it too!

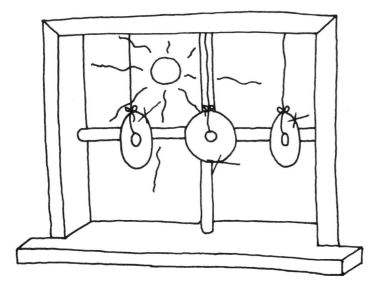

Fun & Fast Fact
Audio CDs (compact discs) were introduced in Japan and Europe in 1982, and in the United States in 1983.

CD Sun Catchers

Materials: 2 compact discs
glue
fishing line
stickers (optional)
glitter (optional)
glue (optional)

Directions: First, glue the 2 CDs together, with the shiny sides facing outward. Use the free internet CDs you get in the mail—not Mom and Dad's favorite music CDs! Thread the fishing line through the hole and tie off for hanging. You can decorate your sun catcher with shiny stickers, or squeeze glue onto the sun catcher and sprinkle glitter onto the glue. Shake off excess glitter for an eye-catching surprise.

Cereal Box Puzzles

Materials: empty cereal box
scissors
resealable plastic baggie

Directions: First, cut out the front or back panel of the cereal box, whichever is the most visually attractive. Next, cut the panel into interlocking pieces. Make larger pieces for younger children; smaller, more difficult puzzles for the older children. Store your puzzle pieces in a resealable plastic baggie so they won't get lost. This is a portable activity, perfect for long waits in the doctor's office.

Fun & Fast Fact
The world's first jigsaw puzzle was made by a mapmaker in 1760. Maps were glued onto a sheet of wood and then cut into small pieces.

Paper Plate Pouch

Materials: 2 paper plates
scissors
stapler
yarn
single hole punch
decorations

Directions: First, cut one plate in half. Now staple a half, to the full plate, forming a pouch. Decorate the pouch with markers, glitter and stickers. Punch two holes near the top of the full plate, and thread the yarn through the holes. Tie the ends. Make the yarn short enough so that it is a hand-held pouch. This is a handy holder for small drawings and paintings.

Fun & Fast Fact
The most expensive perfume is Parfum VI at $71,380! The bottle is made with platinum, gold, rubies and diamonds.

Felt Car Freshener

Materials: felt scraps
scissors
single hole punch
glue
string
essential oil (cinnamon, pine, vanilla, etc.)

Directions: Cut shapes from the felt scraps to form a flower, smiley face, or any other favorite design. Make a hole near the top of your shape and attach a piece of string. (Form a loop with the string large enough to fit around the rear view mirror of a car.) Next, add a few drops of essential oil to your creation and hang it in the family car. A sweet-smelling gift for someone you love.

Wish Can

Materials: clean coffee can with lid
construction paper
magazine cut-outs (optional)
glue
markers

Directions: Cover the outside of the can with construction paper, and glue into place. Decorate the outside of the coffee can with pictures of things you have been wishing for: a bicycle, skates, CD player, dolls. Label the can "My Wish Can." Fill the can with money from allowances, birthdays, and even change found under sofa cushions. This is a fun way for children to learn the importance of saving money.

Fun & Fast Quote
"I don't know much about being a millionaire, but I'll bet I'd be a darling at it."
—Dorothy Parker

Button Flowers

Materials: construction paper
scissors
buttons
chenille stems (green for stems of flowers)

Directions: Cut out flower shapes from the construction paper. Choose a button that matches your flower, and center the button in the middle of the flower. Poke a green chenille stem through the flower, making the stem come up through one hole, then poke it down through the next hole in the button. Twist the ends of the stems together to form the stem of your flower. This makes a colorful gift for Mother's Day that will never wilt.

Fun & Fast Riddle
Q: What kind of button won't unbutton?

A: A bellybutton!

Fun & Fast Fact
The original 8-count box of Crayola crayons cost a nickel 1903.

Crayon Cards

Materials: oven
crayons
small cheese grater or
crayon sharpener
waxed paper
metal cookie sheet
construction paper
metal tongs
oven mitt

Directions: Preheat the oven to 300 degrees. Make shavings by grating or sharpening the crayons. Place a sheet of waxed paper, wax side up, on the cookie sheet and scatter the shavings onto the waxed paper. The more colors you use, the more colorful your picture will be. Place the cookie sheet into the oven. When the colors begin to melt and swirl together, remove the cookie sheet with an oven mitt, and turn off the oven. Place a sheet of construction paper lightly onto the melted crayon. Use the metal tongs to lift the paper and lay it, color side up, to dry. Don't forget to display your artwork for friends and family to enjoy.

Can Carriers

Materials: potato chip can or mixed nuts can with lid
ribbon
single hole punch
stickers (optional)
magazine cut-outs (optional)
glue (if using cut-outs or other decorations)

Directions: Punch a small hole in each side of the can, near the top. Thread a piece of ribbon through the holes and tie in a knot or a bow at the top. Fill with markers, drawing pencils, rolled up artwork, candy, or whatever you choose. Decorate your carrier with colorful stickers or magazine cut-outs. Who knows? You could start a new trend!

Fun & Fast Tip
Take your can carrier with you on vacation and use it to collect mementos from your trip!

Fun & Fast Trivia

Q: Which 7 colors are found in rainbows?

A: red, orange, yellow, green, blue, indigo, violet.

Handprint Rainbow

Materials: rainbow colors
of construction paper
pencil
scissors
glue

Directions: Trace your hand on a sheet of construction paper. (You can simply trace your hand once and stack the other sheets of paper behind the traced sheet and cut all at once, or trace each sheet individually.) Cut along the traced lines. Glue the hands together, with the heel of one hand as the base, then glue the heel of another hand onto the fingertips. Form the arc shape of a rainbow with the hands. A colorful rainy-day boredom buster!

Fashion Jewelry

Materials: multi-colored chenille stems
fancy and decorative shank buttons
wire cutters or strong scissors

Directions: Cut chenille stems into 4-inch pieces. Thread a fancy button onto a chenille stem and center the button. Wrap the stem around your finger to shape it into a ring. Twist the ends of the stem to set the size. Remove the ring and trim away any excess wire. Wrap the ends around the ring to secure the edges. For a bracelet, use a longer piece of chenille stem and several buttons. Show off your creations with a fashion show! See Chapter 8, page 97.

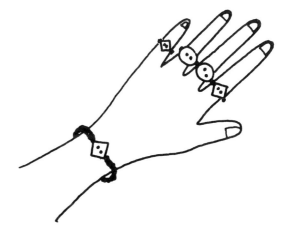

Fun & Fast Fact
The Dresden Green (41 carats) is the world's largest natural green diamond.

Looney Laces

Materials: flat white shoelaces
multi-colored permanent markers
piece of cardboard or plastic bag to use as a drop cloth

Directions: Cover your work area with a piece of cardboard or plastic. Place a shoelace flat on your work surface and use the markers to draw designs, squiggles, and patterns. Don't hold the marker in one place too long because the color will bleed through to the other side. Flip the shoelace over and duplicate your designs. Thread the laces into your favorite pair of sneakers and show off your fancy feet!

Fun & Fast Trivia
Q: What is the plastic covering on the end of a shoelace called?

A: an "aglet"

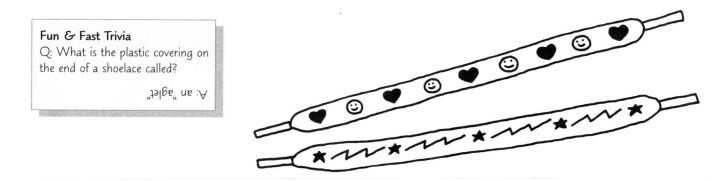

Refrigerator Magnets

Materials: magnetic sheet with self-adhesive side (works well with business card size)
decorations: stickers, beads, pictures, etc.

Directions: Remove the plastic strip from the self-adhesive side of the magnet. Place stickers, beads, pictures or any small decoration of your choice onto the sticky side of the magnet. This adds flare to the Refrigerator Art and Grades Hall of Fame.

Fun & Fast Fact
The world's largest magnet collection contains more than 26,000 magnets! They were collected by Louise J. Greenfarb, "The Magnet Lady."

What can you do? Can you...

• do continuous cartwheels around the yard?

• walk on your hands?

• write and star in your own play?

• choreograph a dance routine?

• make 10 different funny faces?

8: Music, Movement and Mayhem

Dance, sing a song, or just act silly. It's up to you!

Fun & Fast Fact
The largest bottle orchestra was made and played by Patricia Rentner and Roselyn Smith in October 2000. The orchestra consisted of 470 bottles!

Water Orchestra

Materials: 4 or more empty glasses
water
spoon
food coloring (optional)

Directions: Line the glasses in a row on the kitchen table. Next, pour water into each glass; the first glass will have only an inch of water, then vary the amounts for the remaining glasses until the last glass is almost completely full. Add a drop or two of food coloring into each glass. Now gently tap each glass with the spoon. Each makes a different sound!

Tambourines

Materials: 2 paper plates
stapler
uncooked beans, rice, or a few coins
markers
2 metal pie tins (optional)

Directions: Staple the paper plates together, open sides facing each other. Leave a small opening, and pour the uncooked beans, rice, or coins into the opening. (You can make a tambourine for each of these items, to vary the sound that each tambourine makes.) Staple the opening shut. For louder music, use metal pie tins instead of paper plates. Now decorate the outside and jingle away!

Fun & Fast Fact
In the 1400s, Turkish soldiers called Janissaries, played tambourines in military bands.

Karaoke Show

Materials: radio, cassette or CD player
spoon or brush for microphone
silliness

Directions: Find a song that everyone in the family knows. Take turns getting "on stage." Don't be shy! Sing into that brush like you really mean it! For even more silliness, make up new words to an old song.

Fun & Fast Trivia
Q: What is the most widely sung song in the English language?

A: "Happy Birthday to You"

Fashion Show

Materials: adult-sized clothing for girls and boys to wear
accessories: feather boas, wigs, hats, jewelry (optional)
radio
sheet of paper
pencil

Directions: First, help the models get dressed. According to what each person is wearing, write a short description of each outfit onto the piece of paper. Start the music, and announce each model and their clothing to the audience, as they take their turn on the catwalk! This can be a fun way to show off new school clothes, too.

Fun & Fast Fact
On a belt, the loop that holds the loose end is called a "keeper."

Dance Party Invitations

Materials: old compact discs
thin permanent marker

Directions: Make use out of those free internet CDs that you get in the mail! On the shiny side of the CD, write the details for your dance party: where, when, and what to bring. Who wouldn't want to attend a party with such cool invites?

Fun & Fast Fact
The first CD made in the USA was Bruce Springsteen's "Born in the USA."

Dance Party

Materials: compact disc or cassette player
your favorite CDs or cassettes
a few friends

Fun & Fast Trivia
Q: What is the state dance of Illinois?

A: Square dancing

Directions: Invite your friends over for a dance party! Ask each person to bring one or two of their favorite CDs to share with everyone. Dance the night away!

Dancing Streamers

Materials: cardboard tube
different colors of ribbon
glue
scissors
single hole punch

Directions: First, decorate the cardboard tube by wrapping and gluing ribbon around it. Using the single hole punch, punch several holes around one end of the tube. Tie 12-inch lengths of ribbon (or longer) into each hole. Turn on some music and dance, dance, dance!

Indoor "Ice Skating"

Materials: carpeted room or room with hardwood floors
paper plates
wool socks

Directions: Put a paper plate under each foot and "skate" across the carpet! If your house has hardwood floors, wear a thick pair of wool socks to "skate." Who needs ice?

Animal Walk Parade

Materials: radio
silliness

Directions: First, each person in the parade picks their favorite animal. Here's the silly part: Form a straight line, turn the music on and walk and *dance* the way your animal would! If you're an elephant, use your arm as a trunk. Stretch your neck and hold your head up high if you're a giraffe. If you're a bird, flap your wings!

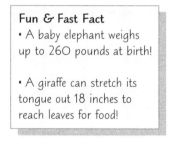

Fun & Fast Fact
• A baby elephant weighs up to 260 pounds at birth!

• A giraffe can stretch its tongue out 18 inches to reach leaves for food!

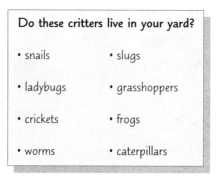

Do these critters live in your yard?

- snails
- ladybugs
- crickets
- worms

- slugs
- grasshoppers
- frogs
- caterpillars

9: Puppets, Critters and Creepy-Crawlies

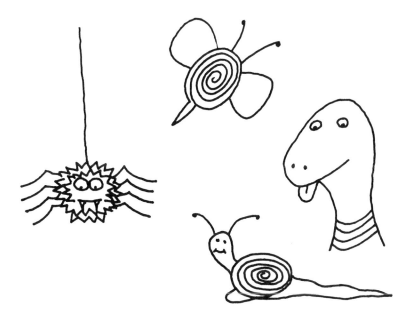

These projects are just for fun—

not for scaring your little sister!

Wooden Spoon Doll

Materials: wooden spoon
markers
yarn
glue
scrap of fabric
ribbon

Directions: First, draw a face inside the bowl of the spoon, using markers. Glue pieces of yarn on for hair. Wrap a small piece of fabric around the handle of the spoon. Tie a ribbon around the fabric, near the bowl to form the doll's clothes. Stir up some smiles with this cute puppet!

Fun & Fast Fact
The red spoon logo for Betty Crocker first appeared on cake mixes in the 1950s.

Sweet Gum Spiders

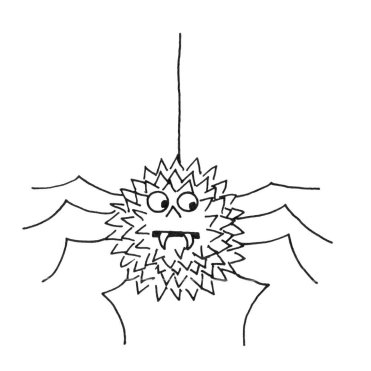

Materials: spiky sweet gum ball
(from sweet gum trees)
black chenille stems
white paper
scissors

Directions: Cut the black chenille stems into 8
pieces, each about an inch long. Now, poke the
stems into the holes of the ball (4 on each side
to make legs). Cut 2 tiny pieces of white paper
into circles and poke onto the sweet gum spikes
(for the eyes). Creepy crawly!

Fun & Fast Fact
The largest spider is the male goliath
bird-eating spider. It was found in
Venezuela in 1965, and had a legspan
of 11 inches!

Lunch Puppets

Materials: paper lunch sack
markers
scissors
glue
accessories (googly eyes, yarn for hair, glitter)

Directions: Draw a face on the bottom of the paper sack. Place your hand inside, with your fingers inside the natural fold. Open your fingers to make the puppet's mouth open and close and "talk." Decorate your lunch puppet with googly eyes and yarn for hair, to make them really stand out.

Fun & Fast Trivia
Q: The largest working puppet, 31 feet 9 inches tall, is a depiction of who?

A: Pinocchio

108

Magnet Dolls

Materials: paper
crayons or markers
magazine cut-outs (optional)
scissors
magnetic cards
glue
metal cookie sheet

Directions: Draw people and animals onto a piece of paper, and cut the figures out. For a faster project, use magazine cut-outs instead of your own drawings. Glue the characters onto the magnetic sheets (or use magnetic cards that have a self-adhesive side). Cut the dolls out again to remove the excess magnet. Place the dolls onto a metal cookie sheet. This is a perfect past-time for those long car rides.

Pretend Ant Farm

Materials: brown construction paper
glue
pencil
fresh coffee grounds

Directions: Draw an ant hill on the construction paper. Squeeze the glue into a long, squiggly line inside the ant hill. Make the end of the glue come out at the top of the hill, then continue squeezing along the edge of the ant hill down one side. Sprinkle coffee grounds onto the glue. Shake off excess coffee and you have a non-biting ant farm!

Fun & Fast Trivia
Q: What is the technical term for an ant farm?

A: Formicarium

Fun & Fast Joke

Q: Why do golfers carry an extra pair of socks?

A: In case they get a hole in one!

Sock Pals

Materials: one sock (kid size or adult)
chenille stem
scissors
uncooked rice or beans
yarn

Directions: First, cut the chenille stem into three small pieces (2 pieces about an inch long, will be used for the eyes, and one piece, about 2 inches long, will form the mouth). The elastic opening of the sock is the hair of the sock pal. Position the mouth piece on or near the toe seam, and insert the ends into the sock. Turn the sock inside out and twist the ends of the stems together. Using the two remaining stems, follow the same procedure to make the eyes. Fill the sock to the heel with uncooked rice or beans. If you are using a tube sock, tie the end into a simple knot, the way you would tie off a balloon. If the neck of the sock isn't that long, use a piece of yarn to tie around the sock, just above the heel. Take your pal wherever you go!

Pet Rocks

Materials: smooth, flat or round rocks
acrylic paints
paintbrush
accessories (googly eyes, glitter, markers, yarn
for hair)

Directions: First, make sure that the rocks are clean and completely dry. Using acrylic paints, paint a face on each rock. For added fun, glue on googly eyes and yarn for hair. Now, name your pet!

Fun & Fast Joke
Q: What would happen if you threw a green rock into a red sea?

A: It would get wet!

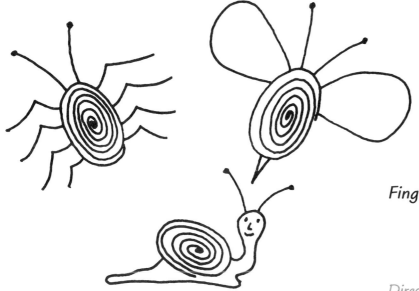

Fun & Fast Fact
Fingerprints are like snow flakes—no two are alike. Even identical twins have different fingerprints.

Fingerprint Critters

Materials: paint or ink pad
paper
black marker

Directions: Press your thumb into the paint, then press onto the paper. This is the creature's body. Now, use a black marker to draw the creature's legs. This is a creepy way to decorate your book covers!

113

Turtle Puppets

Materials: 2 paper plates
white sock
green crayon
black marker
stapler

Directions: First, color the bottom sides of the paper plates completely with the green crayon. Staple the plates together, face to face, leaving an opening on two sides. Next, draw a face (eyes and mouth) on the toe end of the sock with the black marker. Place the sock on your hand and put your hand through the openings of the plates. How fast can this turtle go? As fast as you can!

Fun & Fast Joke
Q: What does a snail say when he rides a turtle?

A: Wheeee!

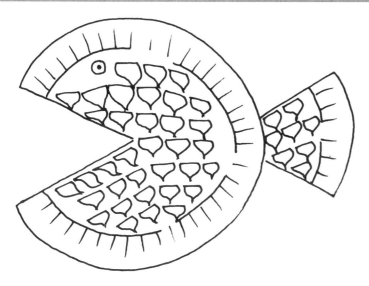

Rainbow Fish

Materials: paper plate
scissors
glue
sheets of different colored tissue paper

Directions: Cut a pie-shaped wedge out of the paper plate. (This will be the fish's tail.) Glue the pointed tip of the tail to the opposite, uncut end of the paper plate. Tear off pieces of colored tissue paper and glue them to the body and tail. For a more textured look, crumple the pieces of tissue paper before gluing them onto the plate. Have you ever seen such a beautiful fish?

Fun & Fast Fact
Fish eggs are one of the most expensive foods in the world. Not just any fish eggs, though. Caviar is made from sturgeon eggs.

Need an excuse to celebrate?

Make up your own wacky holidays by visiting Celebrate Today at www.celebratetoday.com

• March 18 Pillsbury Dough Boy birthday

• April 11 Chocolate for Health Day

• June 4 National Yo-Yo Day

• July is National Anti-Boredom Month

10: Celebrations Using Your Imagination

Make every day a holiday

with party favors and hand-made gifts!

Beaded Valentine Hearts

Materials: 1 red chenille stem
wire cutters or strong scissors
20-30 red tri-beads

Directions: Cut the chenille stem in half or to a length
of 6 inches. Bend one end of the stem slightly, so the
beads will not fall off as you put them on. Thread all
the beads onto the chenille stem and bend the ends of
the stem together. Trim any excess wire and bend the
edges so they will not scratch you. Now, bend the
beads into a heart shape and give to your sweet
valentine.

Fun & Fast Fact
In the 1700s, Englishwomen wrote men's names on scraps
of paper and rolled each piece in clay. They dropped the
pieces of clay into water. The first paper that rose to the
surface, supposedly bore the name of a woman's true love.

Fun & Fast Trivia
Q: Who was the first woman to run for president of the United States?

A: Victoria Woodhall in 1872

USA Sun Visor

Materials: paper plate
blue and white construction paper
scissors
glue
red crayon

Directions: Cut the center out of the paper plate, leaving the rim intact. Color one side of the rim with the red crayon. Now, cut a visor shape from the blue construction paper and glue it to the rim. Cut star shapes from the white construction paper and glue them onto the blue visor. Patriotic and practical!

119

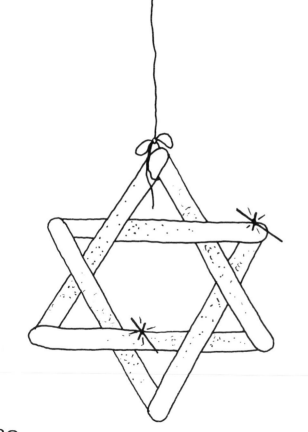

Star of David Decoration

Materials: 6 popsicle sticks
glue
blue glitter (optional)
piece of yarn or ribbon

Directions: Glue 3 popsicle sticks into the form of a triangle. Glue the other 3 popsicle sticks to make another triangle. Now place the triangles on top of each other to form the Star of David, and glue them together. Allow the glue to dry. For decoration, spread a layer of glue along the star and sprinkle with glitter. Tie a piece of yarn or ribbon to the star to hang as a decoration.

Fun & Fast Tip
Create a festive atmosphere by displaying several stars in windows and on walls.

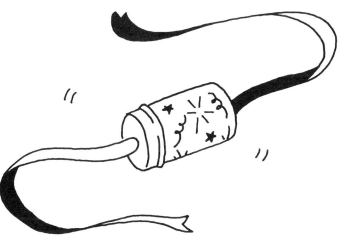

New Year's Noise Makers

Materials: empty film canister
small Phillips-head screwdriver
popcorn kernels
ribbon
stickers

Directions: Poke a hole in the bottom of the canister, and in the canister lid with the screwdriver (a grownup's job). Thread a piece of ribbon through the lid and tie in a knot on the underside. Do the same for the canister itself, making sure the knot is on the inside. Pour popcorn kernels inside and replace the lid. Decorate with bright and shiny stickers, and get ready to make some noise!

Chenille Snowflakes

Materials: chenille stems
wire cutters or strong scissors
string for hanging
colored beads (optional)

Directions: Cut 2 chenille stems to equal length and twist them together in their middles. Spread the stems so they form a "plus" sign. Cut 4 smaller stems and twist one around each end of the plus. For a more colorful ornament, thread beads onto the stems before adding the smaller chenille pieces to the ends. Add a string for hanging from the Christmas tree. Just like real snowflakes, no two are alike.

Fun & Fast Quote
"Cats are smarter than dogs. You can not get 8 cats to pull a sled through snow."

—Jeff Valdez

Cotton Ball Chicks

Materials: 2 yellow cotton balls (or 2 white cotton balls and a yellow washable marker)
black construction paper
orange construction paper
single hole punch
glue
scissors
cup from white egg carton

Directions: If using white cotton balls, paint them yellow with a yellow washable marker. Glue one cotton ball into the bottom of the egg cup. Glue the other cotton ball on top of the first, to form the chick's head. Use the hole punch to make eyes from the black construction paper. Cut a small triangle from the orange construction paper and fold it in half to form the beak. Glue the eyes and beak in place. This makes a cute Easter table decoration!

Fun & Fast Thought
What did the first person to eat chicken say that it tasted like?

123

Fun & Fast Fact
The 7 principles of Kwanzaa are:
Umojo (unity)
Kujichagulia (self-determination)
Ujima (collective work)
Ujamaa (cooperative economics)
Nia (purpose)
Kuumba (creativity)
Imani (faith)

Kwanzaa Necklace

Materials: yarn
red, black, and green beads
scissors

Directions: Cut a piece of yarn for the length of your necklace, and tie a knot at one end so the beads will not fall off. String three red beads (symbolizes blood and the struggle for freedom), three black beads (symbolizes unity), and three green beads (symbolizes the land of Africa) onto the yarn. Keep adding sets of each color, in the order of red-black-green, until your necklace is full. Knot the ends of the yarn together. Present to a loved one as a zawadi (pronounced Sah-wah-dee), or handmade gift.

Mother's Day Fond Memories Jar

Materials: clean mason jar with lid
index cards
markers
square piece of decorative fabric
scissors

Directions: First, cut the index cards in half twice to make 4 small rectangles. On each rectangle, write a special memory of your mother or grandmother. Some questions to ask yourself: How has she inspired you to follow your dreams? What interests or hobbies do the two of you share? Do certain flowers remind you of her? Think of as many special memories as you can. When you're finished writing, fold the rectangles in half and drop them into the jar. Place the square of decorative fabric between the rim and flat portion of the lid and secure. This heart-warming gift will make your mother or grandmother feel special and loved.

Fun & Fast Fact
Thanks to Anna Jarvis, Mother's Day became a national holiday in 1914.

125

Fun & Fast Fact
In the U.S., the greatest number of collect calls made on a holiday happen on Father's Day!

Father's Day Top 10 Lists

Materials: pad of paper
pen

Directions: Make a separate Top 10 list on each sheet of paper. Some topic ideas are "Top 10 Reasons Why My Dad Is The Best"; "Top 10 Things That Make My Dad Smile"; "Top 10 Things My Dad Has Taught Me." When you're finished, place the lists around your house where Dad can find them during his special day. You can place one on his pillow, so he can begin his day with a smile. Maybe another taped to the bathroom mirror, another on the refrigerator door, the front seat of his car—put them everywhere!

Patriotic Jellybeans

Materials: glass mason jars with lids
(various sizes)
red jellybeans
white jellybeans
blue jellybeans

Directions: Start with a small jar, such as a baby food jar, and fill with jellybeans. Make a layer of blue beans on the bottom, then white, and top that with a layer of red. Be sure to count the jellybeans as you add them, and write the number on a piece of paper. Repeat this process with increasingly larger jars, or use only one really big jar. At your next family picnic, have people try to guess the number of jellybeans in each jar. The person who wins walks away with the candy!

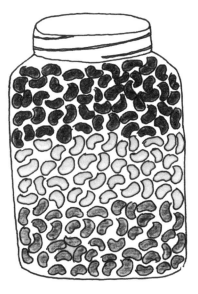

Fun & Fast Trivia
Q: Which flavor of Jelly Belly jellybeans was created for President Ronald Reagan?

A: Blueberry

127

Minimal Mummy

Materials: rolls of toilet paper

Directions: This is a super simple Halloween costume. Have someone wrap you in toilet paper: cover your legs, torso, arms, neck and face. Wrap the paper only once around your mouth and nose, so you can breathe easily. Leave a small opening for your eyes. This is a perfect costume because one size fits all!

Fun & Fast Joke
Q: What's a mummy's favorite music?

A: Wrap music!

Kitchen Safety Tips:

• Always wash your hands before preparing food.

• Wear an apron to protect your clothing.

• Ask a grownup to help with recipes that call for chopping or cutting with a knife.

• Ask an adult to handle anything hot from the oven or stove.

11: Cooking and Munching In the Kitchen

Solve those after-school hunger and boredom blues!

Gummy Jell-O®

Materials: instant Jell-O®
(prepare as suggested on the package)
gummy candies such as worms or
bears

Directions: Prepare Jell-O® as instructed on the
package. After it chills for a few minutes, pour in
gummy worms or bears and mix with a spoon.
Now, chill in the refrigerator until the mixture is
firm. "Excuse me waiter, but there is a worm in
my Jell-O®!"

Fun & Fast Trivia
Q: What are the names of the 6 Gummi Bears?

A: Gruffi, Cubbi, Tummi, Zummi, Sunni and
Grammi

132

Colored Ice

Materials: ice tray
water
different colors of food coloring

Directions: Fill the ice tray with water. Add a few drops of food coloring into each square, and place the tray into the freezer. For kids who don't drink enough water, this may do the trick! Or, drop a few cubes into bath water for even more fun!

Fun & Fast Trivia
Q: What does "mageiricophobia" mean?

A: The intense fear of cooking

Candy Necklace

Materials: licorice string or yarn
circular cereal such as Cheerios® or Fruit Loops®
circular candy such as Life Savers®

Directions: Thread the licorice through the holes in the cereal and candy. Continue adding treats until you have enough to fill your necklace. Tie the ends of the licorice or yarn together for a beautiful and yummy treat!

Fun & Fast Fact
Life Savers were invented in 1912 by Clarence Crane, a chocolate manufacturer.

No-Bake Banana Crunch Cookies

Materials: bananas
graham crackers
resealable plastic bag
butter knife
rolling pin

Directions: Place three or four graham crackers into the plastic bag, and crush the crackers with the rolling pin. Slice the bananas into small circles and drop the pieces into the bag. Shake the bag, coating each slice with crumbs. This simple treat is sure to be a favorite!

Fun & Fast Trivia

Q: Who made the longest banana split in the world?

A: The residents of Selinsgrove, Pennsylvania made it on April 30, 1988. Their banana split measured 4.55 miles long! I wonder how long it took them to eat it?

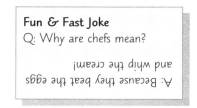

Fun & Fast Joke
Q: Why are chefs mean?

A: Because they beat the eggs and whip the cream!

Whipped Cream Letters

Materials: whipped cream
clean cookie sheet

Directions: Spray or spoon whipped cream onto a clean cookie sheet. Spread evenly. Now, draw letters with your finger. Have your child trace your letters, then try to draw her own. Learning never tasted so good!

Bread Art

Materials: white bread
food colorings
small drinking cups
milk
new paintbrush
toaster

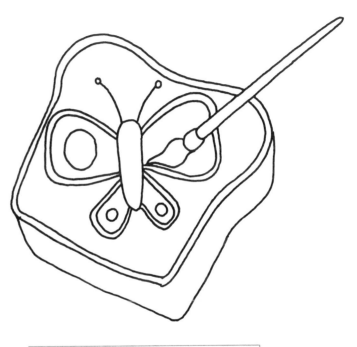

Directions: You will need a drinking cup for each color you wish to use. Pour a small amount of milk into each drinking cup. Add a few drops of food coloring to each cup (a different color for each). Using the paintbrush, paint designs or pictures onto the bread. Don't soak the bread—use just enough "paint" for the picture to show up. Now toast the bread for edible art!

Fun & Fast Thought
What was the best thing *before* sliced bread?

137

Yummy Finger Painting

Materials: package of instant vanilla pudding (prepare as suggested on the label)
food coloring
muffin pan
paper plates

Directions: Spoon the pudding into a clean muffin pan. Add drops of different food coloring to each muffin cup (mix 2 different colors together to make wilder colors). Stir each cup until the color is consistent. Dip your fingers into the colors and "paint" designs onto the paper plates. Yummy!

Fun & Fast Fact
The world's largest finger painting measured 28x35 feet! 200 children in Gaithersburg, Maryland created it on July 19, 1999...but it wasn't painted with pudding!

Popsicles

Materials: pitcher of Kool-Aid®
plastic ice tray
plastic wrap
toothpicks

Directions: Fill a plastic ice tray with flavored Kool-Aid®. Stretch a sheet of plastic wrap over the ice tray and poke a toothpick through each square. Freeze and enjoy!

Fun & Fast Fact
The first ice cream cone was seen at the 1904 World's Fair in St. Louis. A waffle vendor rolled a waffle into a cone shape for an ice cream vendor at the next booth.

139

Fun & Fast Fact
Before rubber came into use, pieces of bread were used to erase lead pencil.

Sandwich Shapes

Materials: bread
peanut butter and jelly (or your child's favorite sandwich fillings)
cookie cutters

Directions: Prepare the sandwich as you normally would. Now, press a cookie cutter into the sandwich and pull out a fun and tasty treat! Toddlers will love this snack!

Munchable Mix

Materials: M&M's®
peanuts
banana chips
raisins
Goldfish® crackers
pretzels
plastic baggie

Directions: Fill a plastic baggie with your favorite munchies. It's the perfect munchable mix for those long car rides!

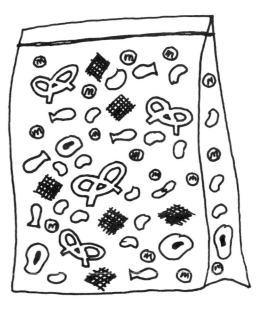

> **Fun & Fast Fact**
> When were your favorite snacks invented?
> Popcorn: 3000 B.C., Americas
> Animal Crackers: 1890s, England
> Cookies: 3rd Century, Rome
> Pretzels: 610 A.D., Northern Italy
> Peanuts: 1800s, United States

Outdoor Safety Tips:

• Wear a sunscreen with an SPF 15 or greater.

• Wear sunglasses (not toy glasses) to protect your eyes from harmful rays.

• Wear light-colored cool clothing on hot days. Bundle up when it's cold.

• Keep plenty of insect repellent on hand.

• Always drink plenty of water.

• On hot days, take breaks every 30 minutes.

12: Outside Fun Guide

Put the remote control down
and get ready for some real fun!

Pine Cone Bird Feeder

Materials: large pine cone
vegetable shortening or suet
peanut butter
cornmeal (optional)
birdseed
bowl
string or yarn

Directions: First, tie a piece of string or yarn to the pine cone. Cover the cone with this mixture: Mix shortening or suet with peanut butter and cornmeal. You can also add dried, chopped fruit or chopped nuts. Next, roll the pine cone in birdseed. Hang the cone from a tree branch outside, preferably one near a window of your home, so you can watch the birds eat.

Fun & Fast Joke
Q: Why are birds poor?

A: Because money doesn't grow on trees!

144

Fun & Fast Fact
Hummingbirds can flap their wings 70 times every second!

Nature Log

Materials: small notebook
pencil

Directions: Observe the animals that visit your pine cone feeder, and keep track of them in your nature log. What kinds of birds visit? If they stay for a while, try to draw their picture, or take notes on what color they are and how many of the same bird enjoy the peanut butter treat. Do squirrels and other critters visit too?

145

Giant Bubble Blower

Materials: wooden dowel (12")
piece of thin rope (24")
bubble solution (see page 39)
bowl

Directions: Tie one end of the rope to the end of the dowel. Now, tie the other end of the rope to the opposite end of the dowel, leaving enough room to hold the stick. Dip the entire blower into the solution (except the part you hold) and turn in slow circles or run through the yard! Heads will definitely turn to see these giant bubbles floating on air!

Rain Stick

Materials: cardboard tubes
waxed paper
2 rubberbands
toothpick
uncooked beans, rice, or pasta

Directions: Cover one end of the cardboard tube with waxed paper and close it off with a rubberband. Pour a handful of uncooked beans, rice or pasta into the open end. Next, cover the open end with waxed paper and another rubberband. Poke holes in the tube using a toothpick. Shake the tube for a "rain shaker" sound. Add flair to your rain stick with paint, stickers, markers, glitter or other decorations. It might be a good idea to have an umbrella handy!

Fun & Fast Fact
The driest place on earth is the Atacama Desert in Chile. The average annual rainfall is 0.004 inches. Some parts of the desert haven't had any rain for over 500 years!

147

Scavenger Hunt

Materials: objects that are found in your favorite story book
paper
pencil
empty sack

Directions: First, make a list of all the items in the scavenger hunt, and give a copy to each child. You don't have to hide the objects as with an Easter egg hunt, though. For example, place objects visibly in trees or on top of bushes, etc. Younger children will enjoy searching for objects that appear in their favorite picture book. Vary the game for older children. This is a fun activity for birthday parties!

Fun & Fast Quote
"You got to be careful if you don't know where you're going, because you might not get there."
—Yogi Berra

Scavenger Hunt!
1 Broom
2 Hammer
3 Basketball
4 Teddybear
5 Baseball Cap
6 Work Boot
7 Rake
8 Skates
9 Yo-Yo
10 Bucket

Coffee Can Stilts

Materials: 2, 1-pound coffee cans
screwdriver
rope

Directions: Turn each coffee can upside down, so the plastic lid is on the bottom. Poke two holes, one on each side of the can, near the top (a grownup's job). Next, thread the rope through the holes in the can and tie off inside the can. The tied rope should be just long enough to be held waist-high when standing on the cans. Does the world look different from up there?

Fun & Fast Fact
The first coffee to be sold in sealed tin cans in the U.S. was Chase & Sanborn in 1878.

Fun & Fast Trivia
Q: What is chalk made of?

A: Tiny plankton fossils

Chalk Designs

Materials: white or multi-colored chalk

Directions: Draw pictures on your driveway or sidewalk with the chalk. Create a game of hopscotch or draw pictures of your friends. And don't worry about messing up. One squirt from the water hose will give you a fresh start!

150

Fun & Fast Trivia
Q: Who was the first person to swim across the English Channel?

A: Matthew Webb in 1875

Water Bonanza

Materials: plastic wading pool
sprinklers
water hose
water balloons
squirt bottles

Directions: Make a water park in your own back yard! Fill a plastic kiddie pool with water. Fill water balloons (for older children) and squirt bottles (such as plastic mustard and ketchup bottles) for the younger children. Space each water activity a few feet apart, and beat the summer heat with a water bonanza!

Water Balloon Toss

Materials: balloons
water
2 or more players

Directions: Fill a balloon with water and tie the end closed. Stand 2 or 3 feet away from each other to start the game. The first person tosses the balloon to the other, using a slow, underhand motion. When you catch the balloon, toss it gently to the next player. Every so often, take a few steps back to increase the space between players. Who wins? Who cares!

Fun & Fast Trivia
Q: What was the first character balloon to be in the Macy's Thanksgiving Day Parade?

A: Felix the Cat, in 1927.

Sun Spots

Materials: blueprint paper (available at office supply stores)
small objects such as leaves; flowers; rubberbands; keys; buttons
clipboard
lots of sunshine

Directions: First, attach a sheet of blueprint paper to the clipboard. Place your collection of objects onto the paper. Leave space between each object when arranging. Set the clipboard and its contents outside in direct sunlight for several minutes. Bring your project inside and remove all the objects. Beautiful artwork—compliments of the sun!

Fun & Fast Fact
The palms of your hands and feet cannot get a sunburn because they don't contain pigment.

Fun & Fast Fact
The origins of iced tea go back to the World's Fair in St. Louis in 1904. Richard Blechyden, a concessionaire, couldn't sell hot tea because it was such a hot day. So, he dumped ice into the tea and voila!

Sun Tea

Materials: clean gallon jug with lid
4 single size tea bags
water
plenty of sunshine

Directions: Remove the wrappers from the tea bags and place the tea bags into the jug. Fill the jug with water. Replace the lid and set the jug in direct sunlight. When the color of the water darkens, pour some over a glass of ice and enjoy!

Shadow Tag

Materials: 2 or more players
lots of sunshine

Directions: This game is played much like regular tag, except the "IT" person tries to step on someone else's shadow rather than tag them. It's a guaranteed good time for a sunny day!

Fun & Fast Fact
Thomas Edison, the inventor of the lightbulb, was afraid of the dark!

155

Educational Resources on the Internet:

- U.S. Department of Education
  www.ed.gov

- National Association for the Education of Young Children
  www.naeyc.org

- Canadian Association for Young Children
  www.cayc.ca

- Parenting Coalition International
  www.parentingcoalition.org

Appendix: Family Resource Centers by State

Parent and Family Resource Centers provide support in the form of counseling, parent training classes, special needs assistance, family literacy programs and much more.

Alabama

Lucile Pierce Family Literacy & Resource Center
103 East Ida Avenue
Opp, AL 36467
(334) 493-8888

Special Education Action Committee (SEAC)
P.O. Box 161274
Mobile, AL 36616
(251) 478-1208
www.home.hiwaay.net/~seachsv

Alaska

Child Care & Family Resources: Family Resource Center
520 Harris Street
Juneau, AK 99801
(907) 463-5437

Alaska Youth & Parent Foundation
Family Resource Center
3745 Community Park Loop, Ste., 202
Anchorage, AK 99508
(907) 274-6541
www.aypf.ak.org

Arizona

Buckeye Valley Family Resource Center
215 South 6th Street
Buckeye, AZ 85326
(602) 386-4008

Casa Grande Elementary School District
Family Resource Center
300 West McMurray Blvd.
Casa Grande, AZ 85222
(520) 836-1048

Family Resource Center
2020 West Durango Street
Phoenix, AZ 85009
(602) 252-1539

Flowing Wells Schools
Family Resource Center
Tuscon, AZ 85701
(520) 690-2368

Queen Creek School District
Family Resource Center
Higley, AZ 85236
(480) 987-5988

Tesseract Family Resource Center
4800 East Doubletree Ranch Road
Paradise Valley, AZ 85253
(480) 991-1770

Arkansas

Camden Fairview Public Schools
Family Resource Center
647 Jefferson Drive Northwest
Camden, AR 71701
(870) 836-6279

Family Resource Center
Sheridan, AR 72150
(870) 942-7373

Family Resource Center
922 East Emma Ave.
Springdale, AR 72764
(501) 927-2804

Poinsett County Family Resource Center
507 Liberty Street
Marked Tree, AR 72365

California

ABC Family Resource Center
518 Main Street
Woodland, CA 95695
(530) 669-2430

Brawley Union High School FRC
480 North Imperial Ave.
Brawley, CA 92227
(770) 344-4913

Exceptional Family Resource Center (EFRC)
9245 Sky Park Court, Ste. 130
San Diego, CA 92123
(858) 268-8252
http://edweb.sdsu.edu/efrc/main.html

Family Resource Center
28191 Marguerite Parkway, Ste. 19
Mission Viejo, CA 92691
(949) 364-0500

Family Resource Center
1178 Broadway
Seaside, CA93955
(408) 394-4622

Family Resource Center
433 Salinas Street
Salinas, CA 93901
(408) 757-7915

Family Resource Center-Healthy Start
4905A 47th Avenue
Sacramento, CA 95824
(916) 394-2040

Legend Learning & Family Resource Center
1690 38th Ave.
San Francisco, CA 94122
(415) 664-1161

Legend Learning & Family Resource Center
1025 South De Anza Blvd.
San Jose, CA 95129
(408) 253-6944

Legend Learning & Family Resource Center
3412 Sierra Road
San Jose, CA 95132
(408) 923-8804

Legend Learning & Family Resource Center
2995 Yerba Buena Road
San Jose, CA 95135
(408) 531-9150

MORE Family Resource Center
1764 Marco Polo Way
Burlingame, CA 94010

Modoc County Office of Education FRC
Alturas, CA 96101
(530) 233-7130

WarmLine Family Resource Center
P.O. Box 160
Rancho Cordova, CA 95670
(916) 631-7995

Colorado

Basalt Family Resource Center
151 Cottonwood Drive
Basalt, CO 81621
(970) 927-8514

Carbondale Family Resource Center
600 South 3rd Street
Carbondale, CO 81623

Colorado Parent Information & Resource Center
1445 Market Street, #350
Denver, CO 80202
(303) 820-5624
www.cpirc.org

Crawford Family Resource Center
1600 Florence Street
Aurora, CO 80010
(303) 340-0880

Cross Community Coalition FRC
2332 East 46th Ave.
Denver, CO 80216
(303) 292-3203

Family Resource Center
355 Adams Ave.
Silverthorne, CO 80498
(970) 262-2472

Holly Hills FRC
4101 East Louisiana Ave.
Denver, CO 80246
(303) 512-0142

South Aurora FRC
1301 South Kenton Way
Aurora, CO 80012
(303) 671-9088

Connecticutt

A H M Family Resource Center
25 School Drive
Marlborough, CT 06447
(860) 295-9731

Child Guidance Clinic for Central Conn Inc. FRC
124 Columbia Street
Meriden, CT 06451
(203) 237-4743

Family Resource Center
482 Norwich Road
Plainfield, CT 06374
(860) 564-1455

Family Resource Center
426 West Main Street
Meriden, CT 06451
(203) 238-2316

159

Family Resource Center
35 Matthews Street
Milford, CT 06460
(203) 874-6822

FRC at Charter Oak School
425 Oakwood Ave.
W. Hartford, CT 06110
(860) 233-4701

Family Resource Center
15 Mercer
East Hartford, CT 06118
(860) 568-0609

Delaware

New Castle County Parent Information Ctr.
700 Barksdale Road, Ste. 16
Newark, DE 19711
(302) 366-0152
www.picofdel.org

Kent County Parent Information Ctr.
1046 S. DuPont Highway
Dover, DE 19901
(302) 674-0184
www.picofdel.org

Sussex County Parent Information Ctr.
109 N. Bedford Street
Georgetown, DE 19947
(302) 856-9880
www.picofdel.org

Florida

Child Care Resource Network
230 North Beach Street
Daytona Beach, FL 32114
www.ccrnetwork.org

Dade County FRC
675 North Homestead Blvd.
Homestead, FL 33030
(305) 245-7169

Drew Charles Family Resource Center
2600 Northwest 9th Court
Pompano Beach, FL 33069
(954) 977-2258

Family Resource Center
10501 FGCU Blvd. South
Fort Myers, FL 33965
(941) 590-7855

Family Resource Center of Citrus County Inc.
120 North Montgomery Ave.
Inverness, FL 34450
(352) 344-1001

Wows Family Resource Center
3600 Rogers Drive
Orlando, FL 32805
(407) 295-1545

Georgia

Bedford Pine Child & Family Resource Center
444 Angier Ave. Northeast

Atlanta, GA 30308
(404) 875-9668

Chatham-Savannah Youth Futures Authority
316 East Bay Street
P.O. Box 10212
Savannah, GA 31412
(912) 651-6810

Family Resource Center
418 Ridge Avenue North
Tifton, GA 31794
(229) 388-1000

Morning Star Family Resource Center
6205 Abercorn Street
Savannah, GA 31405
(912) 691-1262

Morningstar Family Resource Center
408 Tanner
Carrollton, GA 30117
(706) 845-7224

FPRC
P.O. Box 212115
Augusta, GA 30917
(706) 863-3843

Hawaii

Family Support Services of West Hawaii
75-5759 Kuakini Hwy, #203
Kailua-Kona, HI 96740
(808) 329-7773

Family Resource Center
270 Kuulei Road, Ste. 205
Kailua, HI 96734
(808) 262-8800

Kaneohe Community Family Center
46-202 He'eia Elementary School
Kaneohe, HI 96744
(808) 235-7747
www.pacthawaii.org

Kualoa Ecumenical Youth Project
47-200 Waihee Road
Kaneohe, HI 96744
(808) 239-5777

Kuhio Park Terrace Family Center
1485 Linapuni Street
Honolulu, HI 96819
(808) 841-6177
www.hawaiipirc.org

Molokai Family Support Center
P.O. Box 1275
Kaunakakai, HI 96748
(808) 553-3276

Idaho

Idaho Parents Unlimited, Inc.
600 N. Curtis Road, Ste. 100
Boise, ID 83706
(208) 342-5884
www.ipulidaho.org

Illinois

Blossoms Family Resource Center
2002 East 223rd Street
Chicago Heights, IL 60411
(708) 758-4762

Edgebrook Community Center FRC
1926 Green Lane North
Palatine, IL 60074
(847) 776-2523

Ernest Smith Family Resource Center
4731 Tudor Ave.
East Saint Louis, IL 62207
(618) 875-3465

Family Resource Center
20 East Jackson Blvd.
Chicago, IL 60604
(312) 939-3513

Family Resources Center
321 Main Street
Peoria, IL 61602
(309) 637-1713

Mano-A-Mano Family Resource Center
222 East Main Street
Round Lake, IL 60073
(847) 201-1524

Youth & Family Resource Center
4434 South Lake Park Ave.
Chicago, IL 60653
(773) 268-8724

Indiana

Family Resource Center
734 West Delaware Street
Evansville, IN 47710
(812) 425-5214

Indiana Center for Family, School & Community Partnerships
4755 Kingsway Drive, #105
Indianapolis, IN 46205
(317) 205-2595
www.partners-in-learning.org

Indiana Resource Center for Families with Special Needs
809 North Michigan Street
South Bend, IN 46601
(574) 234-7101
www.insource.org

Meadow's Edge Family Connect Center
16333 Kern Road
Mishawaka, IN 46544
(219) 255-9347
http://me.phm.k12.in.us/family_connect_center.htm

Iowa

Anamosa Community Schools FRC
203 Hamilton Street
Anamosa, IA 52205
(319) 462-5318

Central Place FRC
8325 Northeast University Ave.
Runnells, IA 50237

(515) 967-7806

Family Resource Center
211 South Grace Street
Afton, IA 50830
(641) 347-8777

Family Resource Center
321 West South Street
Monticello, IA 52310
(319) 465-3432

Family Resource Center
611 North West
Carroll, IA 51401
(712) 792-6440

People Place Family Resource Center
219 6th Street
Ames, IA 50010
(515) 233-1677

Spencer Community Schools FRC
724 West 9th Street
Spencer, IA 51301
(712) 262-5500

Taylor Family Resource Center
720 7th Avenue S.W.
Cedar Rapids, IA 52404
(319) 398-2084

Kentucky

Benton Central Family Resources
905 Joe Creason Drive
Bentonville, KY 42025
(270) 527-7003

Carr Creek Family Resource Center
P.O. Box 114
Littcarr, KY 41834

Deer Park Elementary Family Resource Center
4959 New Hartford Road
Owensboro, KY 42303
(270) 689-1427
http://daviess.k12.ky.us/dpes/FRC.htm

G.C. Burkhead Family Resource Center
521 Charlemagne
Elizabethtown, KY 42701
(270) 737-0896

Galletin County Family Resource Center
605 East Main
Warsaw, KY 41095

Green County Family Resource Network
412 Durham Street
Greensburg, KY 42743
(270) 932-6097
www.green.k12.ky.us/frc/frc.htm

Hiseville Family Resource Center
P.O. Box 90
Hiseville, KY 42152
(270) 453-4426

Howevalley Family Resource Center
8450 Hardinsburg Road
Cecilia, KY 42724
(270) 862-3287

McDowell Family Resource Center
P.O. Box 264
McDowell, KY 41647
(606) 377-2679

Meade Memorial Family Resource Center
8446 Kentucky Route 40 East
Williamsport, KY 41271
(606) 789-6276

Meadow View Family Place
1255 W. Vine Street
Radcliff, KY 42701
(270) 352-1419

Munfordville Family Resource Center
P.O. Box 939
Munfordville, KY 42765

Richmond Family Resource Center
300 Bond Street
Richmond, KY 40475
(859) 624-4585

Rineyville Family Resource Center
275 Rineyville School Road
Rineyville, KY 40162
(270) 769-9039

Sonora/Upton Family Resource Center
P.O. Box 98
Sonora, KY 42776
(270) 369-8460

South Family Resource Center
Rt. 1, Box 225
Falmouth, KY 41040
(859) 654-3325

Louisiana

East Elementary School FRC
520 Mathilda Ave.
Eunice, LA 70535
(337) 457-5599

Krotz Springs Elementary School FRC
445 Division Street
Krotz Springs, LA 70750
(337) 566-3631

Leonville Elementary School FRC
3774 Highway 31
Leonville, LA 70551
(337) 879-7918

Melville Elementary School FRC
536 Fontenot Street
Melville, LA 71353
(337) 623-3650

Northeast Elementary School FRC
1125 Mamie Street
Opelousas, LA 70570
(337) 942-8322

Southwest Elementary School FRC
898 West Franklin Street
Opelousas, LA 70570
(337) 942-8230

St. Landry Parish Schools FRC
592 Main Street
Sunset, LA 70584
(337) 662-5816

Maine

Advocates for Children Parent Resource Center
157 Main Street
Lewiston, ME 04240
(207) 783-3990
www.advocatesforchildren.net

Maine Parent Federation, Inc.
P.O. Box 2067
Augusta, ME 04338
(207) 623-2144
www.mpf.org

Maryland

Family Crisis Resource Center
107 Washington Street
Westernport, MD 21562
(301) 359-0728

The Family Works
Child Care Connection, Inc.
620 East Diamond Ave., #J
Gaithersburg, MD 20877

(301) 840-3192
www.thefamilyworks.org

Prince George's Child Resource Center, Inc.
9475 Lottsford Road, #202
Largo, MD 20774
(301) 772-8420
www.childresource.org

Massachusetts

Child Care Resource Center
130 Bishop Allen Drive
Cambridge, MA 02139
(617) 547-1063
www.ccrcinc.org

Family Resource Center
(classes, resources and field trips for homeschoolers)
19 Cedarview Street
Salem, MA 01970
(978) 741-7449
http://familyrc.com

First Baptist Family Resource Center
209 Beach Street
Revere, MA 02151
(781) 853-0548

Harwich Family Resource Center
38 Sisson Road
Harwich, MA 02645
(508) 432-5938

Kennedy-Donovan Center Inc. Family Resource Services
9 8th Street
New Bedford, MA 02740
(508) 997-5875

Khmer Family Resource Center
469 Alden Street
Fall River, MA 02723
(508) 673-8818

Southwick Family Resource Center
454 College Highway
Southwick, MA 01077
(413) 569-3456

Michigan

Clinton County Family Resource Center
4179 South US Highway 27
Saint Johns, MI 48879
(989) 224-1436

Family Resource Center
2615 Stadium Drive
Kalamazoo, MI 49008
(616) 343-1651

Keweenaw Family Resource Center
203 East Montezuma Ave.
Houghton, MI 49931
(906) 482-9363

Southgate Community School District FRC
15500 Howard Street
Southgate, MI 48195
(734) 246-7845

Minnesota

Family Resource Center
1400 East Madison Ave.
Mankato, MN 56001
(507) 387-3215

Family Resource Center
519 Oak Grove Street
Minneapolis, MN 55403
(612) 813-5600

Perham Public School FRC
1017 Oak Grove Ave.
Perham, MN 56573
(218) 346-1475

St. Paul Public Schools: Working FRC
350 Saint Peter Street
Saint Paul, MN 55102
(651) 293-5330

Mississippi

Families First Parent Resource Center
119 Front Street
Purvis, MS 39475
(601) 794-5769

Family Resource Center
425 Magazine Street
Tupelo, MS 38804
(662) 844-0013

Missouri

Cape Area Family Resource Center
1000 South Sprigg Street
Cape Girardeau, MO 63703
(573) 334-8170

Center for Family Resources
2770 North Douglass Street
Malden, MO 63863
(573) 276-5500

Family Resource Center
1554 Miller Road
Imperial, MO 63052
(636) 464-9279

Family Resource Center
4900 Swope Parkway
Kansas City, MO 64130
(816) 822-7241

Family Resource Center
300 Carver Drive
Fulton, MO 65251
(573) 592-0178

Family Resource Center
3309 S. Kingshighway Blvd.
St. Louis, MO 63139
(314) 534-9350
http://frcmo.org

Mountain Grove Pre School & FRC
502 East State Street
Mountain Grove, MO 65711

(417) 926-7217

New Madrid Family Resource Center
420 Virginia Ave.
New Madrid, MO 63869
(573) 748-2778

St. Joseph Public School District FRC
514 North 22nd Street
Saint Joseph, MO 64501
(816) 671-4115

Youth & Family Resource Center
118 South Main Street
Windsor, MO 65360
(660) 647-3773

Montana

Child & Family Resource Council
330 East Main Street
Missoula, MT 59802
(406) 728-5437

PCA Family Resource Center
229 East Commercial Ave.
Anaconda, MT 59711
(406) 563-7972

Nebraska

Beatrice Family Resource Center, Inc.
5109 W. Scott Road, Ste. 410
Beatrice, NE 68310
(402) 223-6040
www.frccn.org/Beatrice/index.htm

Columbus Family Resource Center
2402 13th Street
Columbus, NE 68601
(402) 562-6539
www.frccn.org/cct/index.htm

Blue River Family Resource Center
245 E. 9th Street, Ste. 2
Crete, NE 68333
(402) 826-4216
www.frccn.org/Brfrc/index.htm

Dodge County Collaborative Team
835 W. Military Avenue
Fremont, NE 68025
(402) 721-6542
www.frccn.org/Dcct/index.htm

Head Start Child & Family Development
950 S. Burlington
Hastings, NE 68901
(402) 462-4187
www.frccn.org/Hscfdp/index.htm

Phelps County Family Action Support Team, Inc. (FAST)
1308 Second Avenue
Holdredge, NE 68949
(308) 995-4222
www.frccn.org/fast/index.htm

Family Resource Council
4009 6th Avenue, Ste. 18
Kearney, NE 68847
(308) 237-4472
www.frccn.org/kearney/index.htm

Carol Yoakum Family Resource Center
4621 NW 48th Street
Lincoln, NE 68524
(402) 470-0221
www.frccn.org/Yoakum/index.htm

Lincoln Action Program
210 "O" Street
Lincoln, NE 68508
(402) 471-4515
www.frccn.org/Lap/index.htm

Northeast Family Center
5903 Walker Avenue
Lincoln, NE 68507
(402) 471-3700
www.frccn.org/Nfc/index.htm

West Lincoln Family Resource Center
630 W. Dawes Avenue
Lincoln, NE 68521
(402) 436-1987
www.frccn.org/Wlincoln/index.htm

Families Accessing Innovative Resources (FAIR)
704 E. 3rd Street
McCook, NE 69001
(308) 345-2609
www.frccn.org/Fair/index.htm

Nebraska City Center for Children & Families
806 1st Avenue
Nebraska City, NE 68410
(402) 873-4578

www.frccn.org/Ncccf/index.htm

Prevention Pathways
110 N. 7th Street, Ste. 1
Norfolk, NE 68701
(402) 370-3113
www.frccn.org/Prevpath/index.htm

Wesley Center
First United Methodist Church
406 Phillip Avenue
Norfolk, NE 68701
(402) 379-0133
www.frccn.org/Wesley/index.htm

Family Service South
4007 Harrison Street
Omaha, NE 68147
(402) 734-3000
www.frccn.org/Fss/index.htm

Family Resource Library
Children's Healthcare Services
8200 Dodge Street
Omaha, NE 68114
(402) 955-7144
www.frccn.org/CHS_FRL/index.htm

NETWORK, Inc. (Nebraska Families Ethnics Working on Reaching Kids)
3805 N. 16th Street
Omaha, NE 68110
(402) 595-1376
www.frccn.org/Network/index.htm

Omaha Archdiocese Family Life Office
3214 N. 60th Street
Omaha, NE 68104
(402) 551-9003
www.frccn.org/flo/index.htm

Salvation Army Early Head Start
3612 Cuming Street
Omaha, NE 68137
(402) 898-5920
www.frccn.org/Sa_ehs/index.htm

Urban League of Nebraska, Inc. Family Resource Center
3040 Lake Street
Omaha, NE 68111
(402) 451-1066
www.frccn.org/UL_frc/index.htm

Dakota County Interagency Team
801 2nd Avenue
South Sioux City, NE 68776
(402) 494-0601
www.frccn.org/Dcit/index.htm

Wakefield Family Resource Center, Inc.
403 Johnson
Wakefield, NE 68784
(402) 287-2521
www.frccn.org/Wfrc/index.htm

Family Unifying Network, Inc. (FUN)
101 S. 7th Street
Wymore, NE 68466
(402) 645-8252
www.frccn.org/fun/index.htm

Nevada
The Children's Cabinet at Incline Village
865 Tahoe Blvd., Ste. 201
Incline Village, NV 89451

Churchill County School District FRC
690 South Maine Street
Fallon, NV 89406
(775) 428-2600

Pahrump Family Resource Center
484 West Street
Pahrump, NV 89048
(775) 727-3885
www.pahrumpresources.org

Washoe County School District: Sparks FRC
1665 Sullivan Lane
Sparks, NV 89431
(775) 353-5733

New Hampshire
Family Resource Center at Gorham
123 Main Street
Gorham, NH 03581
(603) 466-9018

Grapevine Family & Community Resource Center
Aiken, Antrim, NH 03440
(603) 588-0344O

Upper Room Family Resource Center
Derry, NH 03038
(603) 437-8477

Whole Village Family Resource Center
258 Highland Street
Plymouth, NH 03264
(603) 536-3720

New Jersey
Center for Family Resources
41 Henry Road
Hewitt, NJ 07421
(973) 853-2020

Center for Family Resources, Inc.
12 Morris Road
Ringwood, NJ 07456
(973) 962-0055

Center for Family Resources, Inc.
45 Reinhardt Road
Wayne, NJ 07470
(973) 389-0011

Family Resource Center of Trenton
844 West State Street
Trenton, NJ 08618
(609) 278-4030

Maplewood Family Resource Center
169 Maplewood Avenue
Maplewood, NJ 07040
(973) 313-9289
www.maplewoodfamily.com

New Mexico

Family Resource Center
1601 East Bland Street
Roswell, NM 88201
(505) 623-1496

Oak Tree Family Resource Center
North Highway 41
Moriarty, NM 87035
(505) 832-4030

San Juan College FRC
203 West Main Street
Farmington, NM 87401
(505) 599-0387

New York
Calvary St. Andrews FRC
68 Ashland Street
Rochester, NY 14620
(716) 232-1176

Exceptional Family Resources
1065 James Street
Syracuse, NY 13203
(315) 478-1462

Family Resource center of Rochester
426 Lyell
Rochester, NY 14606
(716) 271-6840

Jennie MOSE Family Resource Center
7 Cleveland Drive
Addison, NY 14801

(607) 359-3839

Nassau County Family Resource Center
160 Old Country Road
Mineola, NY 11501
(516) 571-1155

West Haverstraw Family Resource Center
71 Blauvelt Avenue
West Haverstraw, NY 10993
(914) 942-3180

North Carolina
Family Resource Center
515 Watson Ave.
Thomasville, NC 27360
(336) 474-1200

Graham County Family Resource Center
P.O. Box 605
Moose Branch Road
Robbinsville, NC 28771
(828) 479-2348

Guilford County Schools FRC
617 West Market Street
Greensboro, NC 27401
(336) 370-8190

Jackson County Family Resource Center
1528 Webster Road (Old Webster School)
Webster, NC 28788
(828) 586-2845

Kannapolis City Schools Family Teacher Resource Center
1300 Glenn Ave.
Kannapolis, NC 28081
(704) 932-7835

Living Water FRC and Preschool
2315 Urban Street
Winston Salem, NC 27107
(336) 650-0633

Pine Knolls Family Resource Center
107 Johnson Street
Chapel Hill, NC 27516
(919) 929-0636

Township Three Elementary School FRC
526 Davis Road
Shelby, NC 28152
(704) 481-1568

North Dakota
Grand Forks Public Schools: Parent Education Resource Center
500 Stanford Road
Grand Forks, ND 58203
(701) 795-2765

Pathfinder Service of North Dakota
1600 Second Ave. SW, #19
Minot, ND 58701
(701) 837-7500
www.pathfinder.minot.com

West Dakota Parent & Family Resource Center
336 5th Street West
P.O. Box 1057
Dickinson, ND 58602
(701) 456-0007
www.dickinson.k12.nd.us/westdakota/default.htm

Ohio
Athens City School District FRC
21 Birge Drive
Chauncey, OH 45719
(740) 797-0025

Bellbrook-Sugarcreek Family Resource Center
22 S. Main
Bellbrook, OH 45305
(937) 848-3810

Clifton Avenue Area FRC
1700 Clifton Ave.
Springfield, OH 45505
(937) 323-0612

Corryville Family Resource Center
240 East University Ave.
Cincinnati, OH 45219
(513) 281-2306

Family Life Resource Center
131 Tremont Ave. Southeast
Massillon, OH 44646
(330) 830-2263

Family Resource Center
390 West Walker Street
Upper Sandusky, OH 43351
(419) 294-4093

Family Resource Center of Hocking County
31630 Chieftain Drive
Logan, OH 43138
(740) 385-2354

Franklin Family Resource Center
10 East 6th Street
Franklin, OH 45005
(937) 746-6601

Human Development & Family Life Education Resource Center
151 Campbell Hall, 1787 Neil Avenue
Columbus, OH 43210
(614) 247-6047
www.hec.ohio-state.edu.famlife

Jamestown Area FRC
16 West Washington Street
Jamestown, OH 45335
(937) 675-2697

Oxford Family Resource Center
5445 College Corner Road
Oxford, OH 45056
(513) 523-5859

Oklahoma

Broken Arrow FRC
802 North Sycamore Ave.
Broken Arrow, OK 74012
(918) 258-6545

Child Care Resource Center
1700 1/2 S. Sheridan
Tulsa, OK 74112
(918) 834-2273
www.ccrctulsa.org

Family Resource Center
505 South Lusk Ave.
Elk City, OK 73644
(580) 243-5913

Family Resource Center
719 North Walnut
Stillwater, OK 74078
(405) 744-6539

Family Resource Center
711 North Bullitt Street
Holdenville, OK 74848
(405) 379-7613

Skiatook Family Resource Center
123 S. Broadway
Skiatook, OK 74070
(918) 396-4108
www.owasso.com/frc

Oregon

Chemeketa Family Resource Center
Chemeketa Community College
4000 Lancaster Dr. NE
Bldg. 50, Rm. 125
Salem, OR 97309
(503) 399-3915

Estacada FRC
200 Southwest Club House Drive
Estacada, OR 97023
(503) 630-2888

Family Resource Center
1010 Northwest 14th Street
Bend, OR 97701
(541) 389-5468

Hart Family Resource Center
136 South 3rd Street
Creswell, OR 97426

Howard Family Resource Center
700 Howard Avenue
Eugene, OR 97404
(541) 687-3612
http://schools.4j.lane.edu/howard/howard.html

Maple Family Resource Center
2109 J Street
Springfield, OR 97477
(541) 747-9618

Oakridge-Westfir Family Resource Center
48119 East First Street, Room #15
Oakridge, OR 97463

(541) 782-3226 ext. 4213

Southern Oregon Head Start FRC
223 Southeast M Street
Grants Pass, OR 97526
(541) 471-3450

Pennsylvania

American Family Services, Inc. FRC
910 North Broad Street
Philadelphia, PA 19130
(215) 978-0611

Family Resources
687 Oneil Blvd.
McKeesport, PA 15132
(412) 673-6830

Family Resources
1700 East Carson Street
Pittsburgh, PA 15203
(412) 381-3609

Family Resource Center of Blair County
2702 Pleasant Valley Blvd.
Altoona, PA 16602
(814) 941-7711

Lancaster FRC
238 Manor Ave.
Millersville, PA 17551
(717) 871-3400

169

Monessen Family Center
422 6th Street
Monessen, PA 15062
(724) 684-4370

Pennsylvania Parents Information Resource Center
P.O. Box 333
Honesdale, PA 18431
(570) 253-5913

Rhode Island

BF Norton School Family Center
364 Broad Street
Cumberland, RI 02864
(401) 726-2030

Bright Horizons Family Center
225 Blackstone Street
Providence, RI 02906
(401) 454-0312

Flynn Edmund School Family Center
220 Blackstone Blvd.
Providence, RI 02906
(401) 421-0422

Laurel Hill Avenue School Family Center
85 Laurel Hill Ave.
Providence, RI 02909
(401) 831-6560

Rhode Island Parent Information Network
175 Main Street
Pawtucket, RI 02860
(401) 727-4144

South Carolina

Family Resources Inc.
69 Robert Smalls Parkway
Beaufort, SC 29906
(843) 521-8400

House Calls Family Resources Inc.
316 West Main Street
Pickens, SC 29671
(864) 878-0004

Lancaster Family Resource Network
307 South Catawba Street
Lancaster, SC 29720
(803) 416-8862

Maranatha Family Center
Highway 9 North
Cheraw, SC 29520
(843) 537-2033

South Dakota

Family Connection
303 North Minnesota Ave.
Sioux Falls, SD 57104
(605) 357-0777

Great Plains Children & Family Center Inc.
6400 West 43rd Street
Sioux Falls, SD 57106
(605) 362-9438

South Dakota Parent Connection, Inc.
3701 West 49th St., #200B

Sioux Falls, SD 57106
(605) 361-3171
www.sdparent.org

South Dakota Parent Resource Network
West River Foundation
2885 Dickson Drive
Sturgis, SD 57785
(605) 347-6260
www.bhssc.org/sdprn

Tennessee

Asbury Family Resource Center
2002 Indian Ridge Road
Johnson City, TN 37604
(423) 434-4900

East Hickman Family Resource Center
5191 Highway 100
Lyles, TN 37098
(931) 670-6617

Family Resource Center
217 Grove Blvd.
Paris, TN 38242
(901) 642-2938

Hillsboro School FRC
284 Winchester Highway
Hillsboro, TN 37342
(931) 596-2968

Lincoln County Dept. of Education FRC
208 Davidson Street East

Fayetteville, TN 37334
(931) 438-1488

Mt. Pleasant Elementary School FRC
600 Locust Street
Mount Pleasant, TN 38474
(931) 379-2096

Oneida Schools FRC
438 North Main Street
Oneida, TN 37841
(423) 569-3303

Watertown Elementary School FRC
741 West Main Street
Watertown, TN 37184
(615) 237-9107

Texas
The Arc of Greater Houston
3737 Dacoma, #E
Houston, TX 77292
(713) 957-1600
www.thearcofgreaterhouston.com

Bright Horizons Family Solutions
2411 Braker Lane West
Austin, TX 78758
(512) 833-7090

Denton Family Resource Center
1316 E. McKinney Street
Denton, TX 76201
(940) 566-1800

El Valle Community Parent Resource Center
530 South Texas Blvd., #J
Weslaco, TX 78596
(956) 969-3611

ESCAPE Family Resource Center
3210 Eastside
Houston, TX 77098
(713) 942-9500

Georgetown Family Resource Center
507 East University Ave.
Georgetown, TX 78626
(512) 930-9888

Partners Resource Network
1090 Longfellow Dr., #B
Beaumont, TX 77706
(409) 898-4684
www.PartnersTX.org

Path Family Resource Center
2301 9th Street
Wichita Falls, TX 76301
(940) 767-3996

Texas Fiesta Educativa Project (P.O.D.E.R.)
1017 N. Main Ave., #207
San Antonio, TX 78212
(210) 222-2637
www.tfepoder.org

Utah

Jordan Family Education Center
8449 South 150 West
Sandy, UT 84070
(801) 565-7442

Vermont
Bellwether School & FRC
1186 South Brownell Road
Williston, VT 05495
(802) 863-4839

Bennington School District FRC
181 Orchard Road
Bennington, VT 05201
(802) 447-7764

Sunrise Family Resource Center
244 Union
Bennington, VT 05201
(802) 442-6934

Virginia
Alexandria Special Education Parent Resource Center
Jefferson-Houston School for Arts & Academics
1501 Cameron Street
Alexandria, VA 22311
(703) 706-4552
www.acps.k12.va.us

Arlington County Special Education Parent Resource Center
2801 Clarendon Blvd., #304
Arlington, VA 22201
(703) 228-7239

www.arlington.k12.va.us/departments/specialed/prc

Colonial Heights Middle School PRC
500 Conduit Road
Colonial Heights, VA 23834
(804) 524-3452
www.colonialhts.net/newweb/admin/ppsprc.htm

Fairfax County Parent Resource Center
2334 Gallows Road
Dunn Loring, VA 22027
(703) 204-3941
www.fcps.k12.va.us/DSSSE/prchomep.htm

George Family Development Center
500 Austin Street
Richmond, VA 77469
(281) 238-7645

Military Family Resource Center
4040 N. Fairfax Drive, #420
Arlington, VA 22203
(703) 696-9053
http://mfrc.calib.com

Washington

Enumclaw Youth & Family Resource Center
1356 Cole Street
Enumclaw, WA 98022
(360) 825-4586

Family Resource Center
16225 NE 87th Street
Redmond, WA 98052

(425) 869-6699

Family Resources of Orcas Island
Eastsound, WA 98245
(360) 376-6406

Family Resources Center East County
Washougal, WA 98671
(360) 835-7802

Lopez Island FRC
Lopez Island, WA 98261
(360) 468-4119

Washington D.C.

Family Education Center of Metropolitan Washington
3230 Pennsylvania Ave. Southeast
Washington, D.C. 20020
(202) 582-1488

West Virginia

Brooke Hancock Family Resource Network
4215 Wells Street
Weirton, WV 26062
(304) 797-7850

Eastern Regional Family Resource Network
550 West Sioux Lane
Romney, WV 26757
(304) 822-5787

Family Resource Network of Roane County
319 Market Street
Spencer, WV 25276

(304) 927-6070

Fayette Family Resource Network
102 East Maple Ave.
Fayetteville, WV 25840
(304) 574-0525

Gilmer County Family Resource Network
113 East Main Street
Glenville, WV 26351
(304) 462-7545

Marshall County Family Resource Network
2200 Marshall Street South
Benwood, WV 26031
(304) 232-5077

Mineral County Family Resource Network
251 West Piedmont Street
Keyser, WV 26726
(304) 788-0780

Mingo County Family Resource Network
325 Liberty Street
Williamson, WV 25661
(304) 235-5607

Taylor County Family Resource Network
501 North Pike Street
Grafton, WV 26354
(304) 265-2404

Tyler County Family Resource Network
228 Main Street
Middlebourne, WV 26149

(304) 758-5046

Upshur County Family Resource Network
79 East Main Street
Buckhannon, WV 26201
(304) 473-1051

Wisconsin
Abbotsford Family Resource Center
100 West Spruce Street
Abbotsford, WI 54405
(715) 223-1436

Almond Family Resource Center
P.O. Box 130 (Almond Elementary School)
Almond, WI 54909
(715) 366-2882

Amherst Family Resource Center
357 N. Main Street (Amherst Elementary School)
Amherst, WI 54406
(715) 824-2206

Childrens Development & FRC
424 Washington Ave.
Oshkosh, WI 54901
(920) 236-6566

Children and Family Resource Center
1134 Martin Luther King Drive
Racine, WI 53404
(262) 633-2611

Family Education and Resource Center
540 North 8th Street

Manitowoc, WI 54220
(920) 682-1742

Family Resource Center
461 East Geneva Street
Elkhorn, WI 53121
(262) 743-1890

Family Resource Center of Adams County
500 North Main Street
Friendship, WI 53934
(608) 339-2868

Family Resource Center of Iowa County
829 South Iowa Street
Dodgeville, WI 53533
(608) 935-7300

Family Resource Center of Portage County
1650 Briggs (YMCA Building)
Stevens Point, WI 54481
(715) 341-3609
www.coredcs.com/~spfrc/index.htm

Junction City Family Resource Center
616 West 2nd Street (JF Kennedy School)
Junction City, WI 54443
(715) 457-4609

Marathon Family Resource Center
100 Spring Valley Drive
Marathon, WI 54448
(715) 443-9900

Prescott Public Schools FRC
720 Saint Croix Street
Prescott, WI 54021
(715) 262-3994

Wyoming
Parent Information Center
5 N. Lobban
Buffalo, WY 82834
(307) 684-2277
www.wpic.org

Canada
Carlisle Play and Learn Support Group (P.A.L.S.)
P.O. Box 186
Carlisle, Ontario LOR 1HO
(905) 689-7742
www.pals-frc.on.ca

Golden Family Center
#7 9th Avenue North
Golden, BC VOA 1HO
(250) 344-2000
www.goldenfamilycenter.bc.ca

Niagara Centre for Youth Care
243 Church Street
St. Catharines, ON L2R 3E8
(905) 688-6850
www.ncyc.com

Child 1st Family Day Care
Quadra Island, BC
(250) 285-2565

http://child1st.8k.com

Family Resource Centre
135 Balmoral Drive
Port Moody, BC V3H 1X7
(604) 461-1167
www.vcn.bc.ca/frc

North Bay Military Family Resource Center
39 Sterling Ave.
Hornell Heights, ON P0H 1P0
(   ) 494-2011 ext. 2053
www.airforce.dnd.ca/22wing/mfrc/intro_e.asp

Ontario Early Years Centres
(See full list below; categorized by area)
www.ontarioearlyyears.ca

Brant
330 West Street
Brantford, ON
(519) 759-3833

Bruce-Grey-Owen Sound
356 9th Street
Hanover, ON
(519) 364-6025

Huron-Bruce
77722 London Road
Clinton, ON
(519) 482-8505

Halton-Milton
917 Nipissing Road
Milton, ON
(905) 876-1244

Oakville
337 Kerr Street
Oakville, ON
(905) 849-6366

Burlington
5353 Lakeshore Road
Burlington, ON
(905) 632-9377

Prince Edward-Hastings
301 MacDonald Avenue
Belleville, ON
(613) 966-9427

Leeds-Grenville
166 Pearl Street East
Brockville, ON
(613) 341-9044

Elgin-Middlesex-London
7 Morrison Drive
St. Thomas, ON
(519) 631-9496

London North Centre
265 Maitland Street
London, ON
(519) 434-3644

London West
785 Wonderland Road South
London, ON
(519) 473-2825

London-Fonshawe
150 King Edward Ave.
London, ON
(519) 668-2745

Perth-Middlesex
35 Waterloo Street
Stratford, ON
(519) 273-9082

Erie-London
230 Main Street West
Port Colborne, ON
(905) 834-9071

Niagara Centre
12 Young Street
Welland, ON
(905) 734-3563

Niagara Falls
2999 Dorchester Road
Niagara Falls, ON
(905) 357-2398

St. Catharines
25 YMCA Drive
St. Catharines, ON
(905) 938-9392

Nipissing
171 Chippewa Street West
North Bay, ON
(705) 474-8910

Parry Sound-Muskoka
64 Waubeek Street
Parry Sound, ON
(705) 746-9522

Ottawa
475 Evered Avenue
Ottawa, ON
(613) 728-1839

Ottawa South
2330 Don Reid Drive
Ottawa, ON
(613) 737-6369

Ottawa-West Nepean
1365 Richmond Road
Ottawa, ON
(613) 820-4922

Ottawa-Orleans
211-210 Centrum Blvd.
Orleans, ON
(613) 830-4357

Ottawa-Vanier
297 Savard Street
Ottawa, ON
(613) 744-2892

Peterborough
201 Antrim Street
Peterborough, ON
(705) 748-9144

Barrie-Simcoe-Bradford
40 Fraser Court
Barrie, ON
(705) 726-9082 ext. 248

Simcoe-Grey
44 St. Marie Street
Collingwood, ON
(705) 446-0816

Simcoe-North
356 King Street
Midland, ON
(705) 526-2456

Nickel Belt
5 Westview Crescent
Lively, ON
(705) 692-5565

Sudbury
319-1 Lasalle Blvd.
Sudbury, ON
(705) 525-0090

Thunder Bay-Atikokan
425 Edward Street North
Thunder Bay, ON
(807) 624-5690

Thunder Bay-Superior North
Dorion Loop Road
Dorion, ON
(807) 857-2943

Essex
236 Cherrylawn Crescent
(519) 736-5113

Windsor-West
3115 College Ave.
Windsor, ON
(519) 255-5226

Vaughan-King-Aurora
140 Woodbridge Ave., Unit 166C
Woodbridge, ON
(905) 856-7300

York North
17 310 Yonge Street
Newmarket, ON
(905) 853-0754

Markham
3990 14th Ave.
Markham, ON
(905) 479-0002

Index

About the Author

Deborah Shelton lives in Houston, Texas with her husband Michael, son Kizer, and their dog Amanda Pooh Bear. She enjoys any activity that brings her closer to her family. Visit Deborah's website at www.fiveminuteparent.com for favorite rainy-day projects, family links and The Five Minute Parent email newsletter filled with fun and fast activities, guest articles, contests, announcements and so much more.

Deborah loves to hear from families! Write to her at

Deborah Shelton
P. O. Box 70285
Houston, TX 77270

Send her an email! deborah@fiveminuteparent.com
Call her! 713-880-8090

Above all, remember this:
No matter how hectic your schedule, you can create small treasures and lasting memories
with your children in just minutes! Have fun!

Give the Gift of Fun!

Additional copies of The Five Minute Parent: Fun & Fast Activities for You and Your Little Ones are available from the publisher. Orders may be placed by phone, mail, FAX, or directly from our website. Purchase orders from institutions and schools are welcome.

YES, I want _____ copies of The Five Minute Parent at $12.95 each, plus $4 shipping and handling. (Texas residents please add $0.81 sales tax per book.) Please allow 15 days for delivery.

My check or money order for $_____ is enclosed. Please charge my

Name _____   Organization _____

Address _____

City/State/Zip _____

Phone _____   Email _____

Card # _____   Exp. Date _____

Signature _____

* Don't forget to include your email address to receive the FREE Five Minute Parent email newsletter!

Please make your check payable and return to: Bayou Publishing • 2524 Nottingham • Houston, TX 77005

Call your credit card order to: 800-340-2034 • FAX: 713-526-4342 • www.bayoupublishing.com